I0796079

Spill the Beans

GLOBAL COFFEE CULTURE AND RECIPES

Lani Kingston

gestalten

How Coffee Became One of the World's Favorite Drinks

This is the story of the all-consuming, centuries-spanning romance we have enjoyed with a simple cup of water infused with the seeds of a fruit from Africa.

The topic of coffee has been explored extensively over the past few decades. Coffee shops selling specialty beans with provenance have proliferated through urban centers worldwide, while coffee-plantation tourism has taken off in coffee-producing countries. But while the understanding and appreciation of coffee have burgeoned, the focus is often quite narrow: on coffee's scientific aspects, origin stories, specialty coffee, or on espresso-led coffee culture.

Yet, as this espresso-led coffee culture has increasingly taken center stage, many stories of other rich, vibrant coffee cultures have often struggled to be told. Espresso coffee is often viewed as the epitome of quality, but there are many other coffee styles that are equally delicious, skillfully made, specialized, and culturally significant. In Ethiopia, people sit together around an open fire, while a woman ceremonially roasts fresh green coffee beans to release their aroma; coffee shops near spice and coffee plantations in India grind fresh cardamom pods into local coffee before they brew.

Societies and foodscapes around the world have been shaped by the introduction of coffee, with local people adopting and nurturing the ingredient until it is an inextricable part of their culinary culture. Everything from brewing styles, beans used, and recipes developed are influenced by cultural, climatic, political, and agricultural aspects. Through the sharing of recipes for coffee, the story of a society unfolds.

While coffee may look different in Vietnam than it does in Yemen, it has the same unmistakable taste beloved worldwide, which helps bind us together. Coffee can act as a common denominator when learning about cultures or time periods that are not our own—a familiar thread through the unfamiliar.

Coffee has also changed our relationship with the dark: the stimulating effect of caffeine allows us to claim more hours of the day as our own. Drinking coffee helped Sufis in Yemen stay awake for night time devotions, and today caffeine fuels the endeavors of busy workers and students. In sixteenth-century Istanbul, coffeehouses promoted nocturnal activities and entertainment. Consumption of coffee has led to increased consumption of the night.

Coffeehouses have also been the backbone of resistance movements through times of political turmoil, from Cairo, to London, to Seoul. Colonialism, imperialism, conquest, and tourism have spread the cultivation of the crop and culture, too (witness the Parisian-style cafés in Hà Nội, Vietnam). Wars were fought, societies were shaped, people were enslaved and taken around the world to work on plantations, their descendants' storylines changed forever. Families emigrated to try their luck farming coffee, while entire cities were built around the ports that supported a bustling coffee trade—cities that still exist today.

It is important to note the ways in which coffee has had a detrimental impact on societies and environments, too, either through its introduction or its →

→ production. Too many producing countries are still subject to neocolonial dominance by wealthy consumer countries or multinational coffee traders and roasters. There are extreme equity issues for coffee workers worldwide regarding working conditions, pay, and living conditions. Coffee production was, for a significant part of history, powered by slavery. Many subsistence farmers were also forced into plantation-style agriculture to provide export crops for their colonial masters; child labor was (and still is, in some countries) common.

The Enlightenment writer J.H. Bernardin de Saint Pierre wrote in his book *A Voyage to the Isle of France, the Isle of Bourbon, and the Cape of Good Hope*, published in 1773, that, "I do not know if coffee and sugar are essential to the happiness of Europe, but I know well that these two products have accounted for the unhappiness of two great regions of the world: America has been depopulated so as to have land on which to plant them; Africa has been depopulated so as to have the people to cultivate them."

Today, many countries, economies, and about 125 million people rely on coffee cultivation and export for their livelihood. We see, through the chapters of this book, how reliance on coffee production has brought both great gains and devastating losses. Climate change, coffee rust disease, and more have already caused devastation to many coffee-growing regions.

Looking to the future, producing countries are also facing a potential geographical redistribution of coffee-growing areas, posing a socioeconomic disaster for the farmers whose lives and cultures are intertwined with their land. The Tanzania Coffee Board expresses a concern that, as the minimum growing altitude for *arabica* increases because of changing climate, damage to ecosystems may be caused by agricultural migration. These are just some of the issues faced by people in coffee-growing regions worldwide.

To ensure coffee has a future, the scientific community is working tirelessly to protect, preserve, and develop the much-loved plant, to ensure our continued daily enjoyment for centuries to come. Scientists are concentrating on discovering new species, working with farmers to increase the sustainability of their crops, testing and breeding climate-resilient varieties, and mapping entire countries to determine the best areas to plant in the future. Their projects have recently been focused on modeling what will happen to coffee as climate change progresses and building solutions.

The way people consume coffee says a lot about who they are: their history, where they come from, their local history of trade and international connection, their tastes and preferences, and what influences they have been exposed to. People all around the world took the seed of a fruit from Africa and made it their own, incorporating their own ideas, techniques, and local ingredients.

Coffee, as simple as it may seem, is a topic with numerous dimensions. To better understand it, we begin our journey by laying down the basics: we introduce you to the coffee plant, how it is harvested and processed, and share key knowledge on how to brew the perfect cup.

The following stories of coffee culture celebrate diversity and innovation. They explore just how interconnected our world is—and how a simple fruit can help to bridge religion, politics, and geographical barriers. Through these stories, you can travel the world from the comfort of your kitchen, as you learn how to make and enjoy these recipes yourself.

Spill the Beans is intended as an exploration of each country's position as a *coffee consumer:* not only their role as a *coffee producer.*

As such, you may wonder why many of the chapters in this book omit key details about growing areas, processing styles, or harvesting techniques used in a country. This is a distinct and intentional diversion from many coffee books. Many on this subject are written to help consumers find a bean they like, or for coffee professionals to discover more about coffee origins. Much of this dialogue around coffee and the countries that produce it, thus focuses on a country's cultivation of a commodity to be consumed elsewhere.

Spill the Beans focuses on how the seed of a fruit from Africa won the hearts of people all over the world, and how they welcomed it into their own unique culinary cultures. As such, it's an excellent addition to an existing coffee library, while also being an approachable introduction to someone just getting into coffee. Many of the recipes are easy to achieve and require very simple equipment. More experienced coffee brewers can brew the base of many recipes with their preferred coffee brewing methods and/or beans, while making small adaptations to experience unique and flavorful brews.

The recipes in this book use a range of measurements listed in metric and imperial, some by weight, some by volume. Coffee is usually brewed by professionals using weight measures and the metric system; however, if a recipe traditionally does not require accuracy, it has been simplified into cup and spoon measures for the ease of the reader.

For recipes that require accuracy, weight measures are often used. You may also find weight measures for liquids (i.e., grams instead of milliliters, ounces rather than fluid ounces). For these recipes, brewing over a scale is necessary for correct extraction and accurate flavor.

The preferred measurement for these recipes is metric, as the imperial system does not allow for accuracy with small quantities of ground coffee. If you do not have precise metric scales (or would prefer to use spoons for measuring out ground coffee) these recipes have approximate U.S. tablespoon measures listed for your convenience, too.

For recipes that do not require accuracy, the whole recipe has been simplified into standard U.S. cup and tablespoon measures. For these, it won't matter if you use U.K. or Australian size cup or tablespoon measures instead.

Ideally, use precise scales (accurate to 0.1 of a gram). One level tablespoon of ground coffee is roughly 5 g, while a heaping tablespoon is roughly 7 g.

LANI KINGSTON is a food writer, researcher, and consultant, with a focus on coffee, chocolate, and sustainable food. She holds Master's degrees in both Food Studies and Education, a degree in Film and Television, and barista and pastry chef qualifications.

Lani has spent years both living in and traveling to many different countries around the world, delving deeply into local coffee cultures and traditions through her work. This, her third book on coffee, summarizes years of research and aims to honor and pay respect to these remarkable coffee cultures.

Hackney Family Cycling's stolen kit found in police raid
Wildlife-friendly reedbed to be planted on the Lea
CITIZEN

Everything You'll Need to Know About Coffee

To successfully brew many of the recipes in this book, you'll need a basic understanding of coffee and brewing techniques.

Many of the countries and regions covered in this book produce coffee. While you'll find entire books detailing the unique characteristics of coffee, and how the flavor profile differs between the various growing regions, the focus of this book is on each country's role as a coffee *consumer.*

Although the sharing of cultural recipes and the particular ways each country brews coffee is the key focus, it is important to note that the main ingredient itself—coffee—differs depending on where it is grown, how it is harvested, what type of coffee it is, and how it is roasted. Below is a quick summary to help you understand how to choose the best coffee for each recipe.

The Coffee Plant

Rubiaceae is a family of flowering plants, of which the genus *Coffea* is a part. There are more than 100 species in the *Coffea* genus, but only a few are relevant to coffee consumers. *Coffea arabica* and *Coffea canephora* (commonly known as *robusta*) are the two most commercially important species.

Coffea canephora (*robusta*) is a popular and sensible choice for many smallholder farmers worldwide. It requires less-intensive maintenance, is less expensive, less susceptible to disease, and more weather resistant than *Coffea arabica*. The higher levels of caffeine and lower sugar content of *robusta* make it less susceptible to pest damage but result in a more intense, more bitter, and less sweet brew, too. *Robusta* is often included in Italian espresso blends because it produces a thicker *crema* (see page 262).

Coffea arabica is considered the gold standard for quality and exceptional flavor. The majority of specialty coffee is *arabica*, although interest in other species is increasing because of their potential for unusual flavors, lower natural caffeine levels, their suitability to particular climates, or their disease resistance. Common tasting notes used to describe *arabica* include fruity and floral, with hints of berries, chocolate, or nuts, reflecting its higher sugar content.

Coffea liberica is the third species with commercial significance, although it makes up only a tiny portion of global coffee cultivation. Like other species, it is native to Africa, although it is cultivated mainly in Southeast Asia, where it was introduced as a fungus-resistant alternative to *arabica* in the late 1800s. It is bolder and earthier than its cousins and often has what some describe as a smoky flavor.

Varieties and Cultivars

You'll come across these two terms as you explore the world of coffee beans. Each coffee species has spawned many varieties over time as they spread around the world. While the terms cultivars and varieties are often used interchangeably, in general, cultivar is used for coffees that have been cultivated, propagated, or in some way influenced by human interaction: a cultivated variety. There are many naturally occurring wild and hybrid varieties of coffee, too, although most of these are not produced commercially.

There are many varieties and sub-types. *Typica* is an *arabica* variety with a long heritage that can be traced back to some of the first coffee cultivated outside of Yemen, on the Malabar coast of India and the Indonesian island of Java. *Bourbon*, a variety of *arabica*, is often prized for its complex, balanced aromas. It developed naturally on the Indian Ocean island of Île Bourbon (now known as Réunion) hence its name.

Caturra, *Catuai*, and *Mundo Novo* are commonly found mutations, crosses, and hybrids of *Bourbon* and *Typica*, developed or cultivated for either pest resistance, flavor, or their higher yields. *Gesha* is a variety beloved for its quality and flavor profile. It is one of the most famous varieties and fetches some of the highest prices at coffee auctions, where green coffee (see page 262) is sold to roasters and buyers around the world.

The Coffee Bean

The coffee bean is actually the seed of the coffee cherry, the fruit that grows on many plants in the *Coffea* genus. These cherries are harvested when bright red, then processed to remove the seeds, of which there are usually two in each fruit. About 4–5 percent of each harvest worldwide will contain peaberries (see page 265), which is the name for coffee beans that grow solo within a fruit. It is thought by some that these coffee beans have a better flavor, as all the goodness transferred from the coffee cherry is concentrated in one bean.

Where Coffee Is Grown

Coffee is cultivated in more than 70 countries, located almost entirely within the humid equatorial region between the two tropics, 25 degrees north and 30 degrees south of the equator. This area is known as the bean belt, and these growing regions have steady temperatures of around 20°C (68°F), rich soil, moderate sunshine, and sufficient rain.

Harvesting Coffee

Coffee is harvested differently depending on the size of the farm, the relative flatness of terrain, the style of coffee, and local cultural norms. Many large farms →

→ employ *Strip Picking*, for which either mechanical pickers or farmworkers harvest all the cherries in a single pass. The beans are then sorted for ripeness using a variety of methods, such as flotation tanks, in which unripe cherries are separated via water channels. In Brazil, where many of the farms are extremely large and the terrain is flat, it is more cost-efficient to mechanically harvest all the cherries in one pass and discard what is not yet ripe, than it is to pay pickers to carefully select only fully ripened cherries.

Selective Picking is employed by many specialty producers, smallholder farmers, or on farms where hilly, rocky, or mountainous terrain makes access difficult for mechanical pickers. This harvesting method is usually thought to result in a higher quality coffee because the coffee pickers are trained to harvest the cherries only when perfectly ripe. The trees will be revisited time and time again as the remaining cherries ripen, ensuring the whole crop is picked at peak ripeness.

Processing Methods

There are two main processing methods that are employed in some variation on most coffee farms worldwide. The *Dry Method*, also known as the natural method, is often employed in regions where access to water is limited, or when farmers can't afford expensive machinery. The cherries are laid out to dry in the sun, where they begin fermentation and are continually raked over a period of days or weeks, until they reach 10–12 percent moisture content. Then the beans will be hulled, using a mill to remove the dried fruit and reveal the bean within.

The *Wet Method*, also known as the washed method, requires a lot of water and specialized machinery. The coffee cherries are immersed in water, sorted, and then pass through a moving press that removes the skin and the flesh of the fruit (pulp). Left behind is the bean covered in mucilage, a sticky layer of the coffee fruit. The beans are fermented in tanks to break down this mucilage (although sometimes, mechanical means are employed to remove it), and the beans are then washed and laid out to dry until they reach 10–12 percent moisture content.

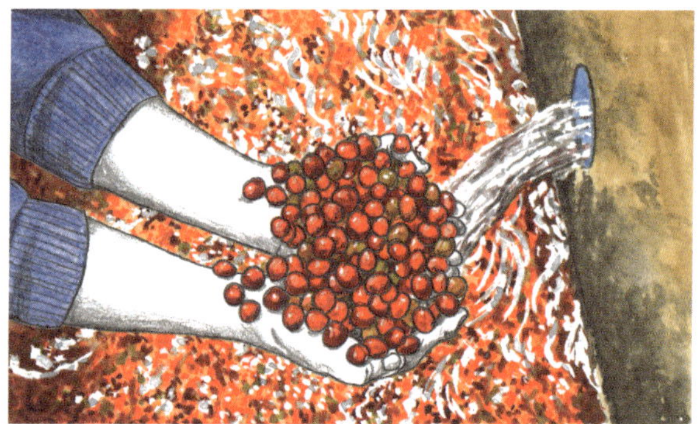

Other processing methods that can be used include *Semi-Washed Methods*, which have become popular in specialty coffee production. *Pulped Natural* or *Honey* are semi-washed methods, where coffee cherries follow the process for the washed method but skip the fermentation stage, with the beans heading straight to be sun-dried with the mucilage still attached. This style of coffee is often known for its sweetness and reduced acidity.

Many farmers, producers, and regions have their own particular ways of doing things, too, using a number of variations on the above basic processing methods. Other farmers are experimenting with different fermentation methods, aiming to coax specific, unique flavor profiles from their coffee through experimental processes such as the adoption of a winemaking technique called *Carbonic Maceration*. In this process, fruit is fermented in a sealed, carbon-dioxide rich environment, creating unusual fruit or wine-like flavors in the coffee.

Roasting Coffee

Coffee, before it is roasted, is generally referred to as green coffee (see page 262). Roasting is key to unlocking the flavors and aromas within the coffee beans. During the roasting process, complex chemical reactions take place within the coffee bean.

Green coffee contains over 250 aromatic molecular compounds, whereas roasted coffee contains more than 800. These aromatic chemical compounds develop as amino acids, sugars, peptides, and proteins, and are combined, created, or destroyed during the roasting process.

Coffee can be roasted from very light through to very dark. As with other food items, the longer it is roasted for and the higher the heat, the darker it will get. In general, the darker the roast, the more bitter the coffee will be, and the lighter the roast, the more acidity the coffee will have.

Color is often used to judge the roast level, on the assumption that the darker the bean, the more it has been roasted—but it is important to note that various coffees will look different, even though they may have been roasted to the same level. For example, Sumatran coffee beans tend to look quite light in color, and could be the same color as a light roast of another type, even if they are actually roasted much darker. A more accurate way to judge the roast level is by the appearance of the bean: the further along the roasting process it gets, the shinier the individual beans will be, as the lipids from the bean's interior move to the surface.

Many of the recipes in the book recommend a specific roast level to use. Choosing the right roast will help you to get a flavor that's closest to what you would find in the recipe's country of origin, though you can also use whatever you have on hand.

Green

Unroasted coffee.

Golden/Blonde

A very light roast, which essentially just dehydrates the beans. Often used for Arabic coffee in the Gulf States. *Tea-like, toasted grain, light, mellow.*

Light

Light brown roast level, which is becoming more common as coffee quality rises. Darker roasts impart the flavor of roasting into the bean, whereas lighter roasts pronounce the inherent flavors in the coffee itself. *Bright, fruity, high acidity, floral.*

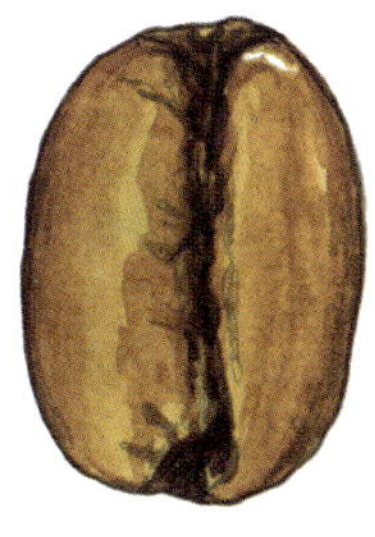

Medium

Sometimes referred to as an American roast, where this roasting level is popular. As coffee passes into the medium-dark range, shininess begins to develop on the outside of the bean. *Chocolate, nutty, sweet, full-bodied, balanced.*

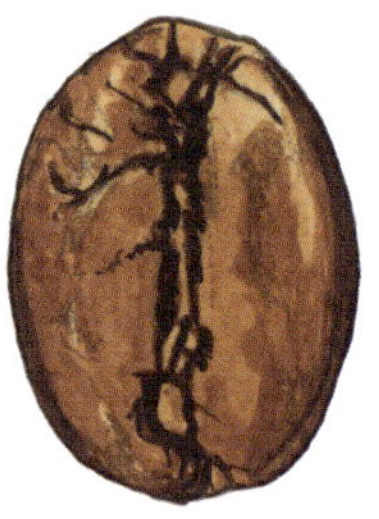

Dark

Dark roasts range from just past medium-dark through to quite charred, with bitterness increasing the longer it has been roasted. Dark roast beans weigh less because of the increased moisture loss, so if measured out by volume rather than weight you'll end up with a slightly weaker cup. *Bold, rich, low acidity, caramel.*

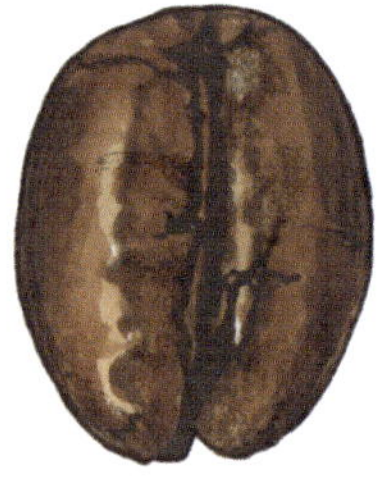

Kopi/Torrefacto/Café Torrado

Sugar roasted beans common in Southeast Asia, Spain, and Latin America. The beans are sometimes coated in margarine or butter, too. *Bitter, dark, intense.*

Selecting Beans

There are innumerable options when it comes to selecting what type of coffee to use: espresso blend, single-origin, *arabica*, *robusta*... Which is the best coffee? The answer is, whatever coffee you like to drink. That's the purpose of this book—to show that there is no single right way to make your morning brew. It's all down to personal preference. If you are a fan of light-roast coffee from Guatemala, you can use that to brew many of the recipes in this book. Dark Italian espresso blends? That will work too.

However, you will find that a number of the recipes call for specific coffee beans. If a style of bean, roast or blend is listed, it means that it is an important component of that recipe. For example, the chicory-blended coffee used for a traditional South Indian filter *kaapi* (see page 96) is necessary for both flavor and proper extraction (the chicory holds onto the water for longer than coffee, leading to a much stronger decoction). You can, of course, attempt the recipe with other beans, but note that you will end up with a different result.

Grinding Coffee

Buying coffee beans and grinding them yourself, rather than buying ground coffee, will result in better coffee; the whole beans will lock the flavors away until you are ready to grind and brew. It's important to grind your coffee beans when they're as fresh as possible, and use them straight away.

There are two types of coffee grinders: burr and blade. Blade grinders are inexpensive, but the longer you grind, the finer the coffee will get. Knowledge and good timing is the only way to grind to the required

level. Blade grinders chop, so they often produce an uneven grind and lots of powder. Blade grinders also cannot generally grind fine enough for espresso or Turkish extraction.

Burr grinders are preferred by coffee professionals. They allow the user to set a specific burr width, allowing the coffee to be pulverized to a fairly consistent size. For the novice coffee brewer, this grinder style (while more expensive) will often come with presets for fine, medium, or coarse, helping you to learn about proper grind size. Don't underestimate the importance of getting your grind right—this is one of the biggest barriers between you and your ideal extraction of a delicious cup of coffee.

The only way to determine the settings on your own machine is through a little trial and error. You might want to use some cheaper coffee the first time, because getting it right will take a bit of experimenting.

Start by turning your grinder to the finest setting. Grind a little coffee. If no coffee comes out of the grinder, set it a little coarser. When you've got the finest grind your machine can handle, rub some of the ground coffee between your fingers. For a fine grind, used for espresso, you are looking for a consistency somewhere in between table salt and flour. If it feels like powdered sugar, congratulations! Your grinder is good enough to grind extra-fine, which is what you will need for Turkish coffee. From there, you'll just adjust the machine to make the grinds coarser, moving into medium and eventually coarse territory.

In this realm, it's mostly about taste. Medium to coarsely ground coffee is used for many immersion coffee brews (see page 16), and you can dial this in based on your own preference. Of course, these flavors are also subject to water temperature and brew time, coffee bean age, and many more factors!

It may be difficult to learn about grind size from the pages of a book, but the key to fine-tuning your grind is this: if your grinds are too coarse, you will under-extract your coffee. This will likely taste sour and acidic, and your brew color may be quite light. If your grounds are too fine, you will over-extract your coffee. It will be dark in color, intensely bitter, perhaps ashy, and you'll have lost most of your sweet, caramelly, or fruity flavors.

Measuring Coffee

Coffee connoisseurs and baristas usually use the metric system and a set of precise scales to measure ingredients. It is very difficult to accurately measure the small quantities required for coffee brewing using imperial measurements. If you would prefer to use imperial measurements, or if you don't have scales, quantities in the recipes have been adapted into U.S. cups, tablespoons, and teaspoons for your convenience.

For recipes that require accuracy to replicate properly, weight measures are used. For recipes that do not require complete accuracy, the whole recipe has been simplified into standard cup and tablespoon measures. For these, it won't matter whether you use the standard U.K. or U.S. size cup or tablespoon measure, even though these measures have slightly different volumes.

When weight measures are listed for ground coffee, a tablespoon measure is given for convenience, too. Note that there are many schools of thought about what a heaping tablespoon is, so, for consistency, the following recipes adhere to these measures: a level tablespoon of ground coffee is roughly 5 g, while a heaping tablespoon is roughly 7 g.

Water for Coffee

Most basic coffee recipes use water that is a minute or two off the boil. As with weight measurements, for the recipes in this book that do not traditionally require →

→ accuracy, water is simply described as hot. This simply means water that came off the boil 30–90 seconds before. You don't need to be too fussy.

Some recipes list a water temperature. These recipes are usually the ones that list ingredients by exact weight, and traditionally require a little more accuracy to brew. You can always brew casually, though, disregarding these extra notes, but following them will help you to get the best flavor from your coffee.

So, do you need to use a thermometer to determine the water temperature? Not always. Everyone's water will cool at a different rate (depending on the volume of the water, what you are boiling it in, and the ambient temperature), but you can do a test in your home conditions and use the results in the future to make brewing easier.

Boil water in your standard appliance, and take a measurement with a thermometer. This should really be around 100°C (212°F) right off the boil, but if you are at a high altitude your boiling point will be lower. After 30 seconds, take the temperature again. The difference between your starting temperature and the temperature after 30 seconds is your cooling rate. So if a recipe calls for 96°C (205°F) water, and you know that your cooling rate is 4°C per 30 seconds: next time, you can just use water 30 seconds off the boil.

Brewing Coffee

The majority of coffee equipment and recipes all extract coffee using one or more of the following primary brewing methods: *pressure, immersion, boiling,* or *filtration.*

Boiling (although a bit of a misnomer, as coffee is rarely brought to a rolling boil with this method) is when both the grounds and the water are placed over heat until the desired strength and flavor has been achieved. *Immersion,* also known as *steeping,* is when hot water and coffee grounds are mixed together and left to sit for a specific length of time. *Pressure* brewing extracts the solubles from coffee beans at high pressure, such as in an espresso machine, and *filtration* methods are those that allow water to extract solubles from the beans and then pass through a paper, cloth, or metal filter to remove the grinds.

Many coffee brewers will employ one or two of these methods. For example, when using a French press, also known as a *cafetière,* your coffee will steep in hot water for a specified amount of time, and then the grounds will be filtered out as you press the filter disc down.

The espresso has permeated coffee culture worldwide. There are a number of different styles and methods for brewing espresso coffee, but they all operate on the same basic principle: hot water is forced under pressure through finely-ground beans to extract a concentrated coffee. An espresso shot is the base of many coffee drinks, but if you don't have an espresso machine, or the desire to invest in one, all is not lost.

Many of the recipes in this book call for black coffee, an espresso, or a liquid measurement of strong coffee. You can really make the coffee for many of these recipes with whatever brew method you usually use, as long as it's of a similar strength (or diluted as required). For example, you can't replace a cup of black filter coffee with a cup of espresso, but you could dilute the espresso with water to make it the same strength.

If a recipe calls for a cup of black coffee, you could make a French press, filter coffee, or simply make a cup of good-quality instant coffee. If a recipe calls for an espresso, you can use an espresso machine, a capsule espresso maker, or a stovetop espresso maker. While capsule and stovetop espresso makers do not produce a "real" espresso, they are a suitable substitute. They make a super-concentrated extraction suitable for use in many recipes that call for an espresso.

Everyone brews coffee differently, depending on where they come from, and what flavor they like, and recipes also differ between regions, cities, and even households. Many of the recipes in this book capture just one of the many ways coffee can be brewed. The following recipes are a good starting point to begin your experimentation, but you are encouraged to research and try different methods, beans, and roasts to find one you like.

A Note on Coffee Strength

Strong is an adjective that is often used interchangeably to describe coffee that is either roasted dark, is intensely flavored, or is high in caffeine. It is important to note that these all mean very different things in the cup. In coffee terminology, strength actually refers to the ratio of extracted solubles to water. This is the percentage of dissolved materials per unit of liquid beverage, or, simply put, how concentrated the coffee is. Dark roasted coffee is not actually stronger, nor is it higher in caffeine, although it may taste stronger because of the intense bitterness that develops over a longer roasting time. Actually, if measured by scoop, light roasted coffees will actually have slightly more caffeine because dark roasted coffee is less dense—so you'll actually be using less coffee per unit of liquid measure.

The Espresso Brew Ratio Debate

When it comes to making espresso, there are many schools of thought and much debate on what's considered the correct way to do things. In practice, though, the ratios and measurements of an espresso differ drastically depending upon taste preference, culture, roast style, coffee origin, grinder type, and more. Lightly roasted single-origin Nicaraguan coffee is going to require different treatment from a *robusta*-blended Italian dark roast.

Traditional Italian ratios use 7 g for a single shot of espresso, 14 g for a double. Many modern specialty cafés use a higher dose, anywhere between 16–19 g for a double shot.

These days, many baristas build their own recipes using their preferred brew ratio. The most common ratio in specialty cafés outside Italy is roughly 1:2 coffee in, to coffee out. This means that, say, 18 g of ground coffee would deliver a double espresso shot that weighed 36 g in the cup. This is typically extracted over 20–35 seconds. In Italy, however, the traditional brew ratio is 1:3 (for a *normale*), or 7 g of coffee resulting in a 21 g single shot. Lower brew ratios (1:2) are considered *ristretto espresso* (restricted espresso), or higher brew ratios (1:4), *lungo espresso* (long espresso).

As always, you will need to experiment to discover what flavor you like best. Try the traditional Italian (1:3) ratio, and from there, you can experiment with other ratios until you find one that works best with your taste preferences and your beans.

Organic or Fair Trade?

Should you choose organic or fair-trade coffee? These, unfortunately, are highly politicized topics that generate varied opinions. While organically grown coffee is most likely better for the environment and for farmworkers, certifications are often difficult to come by, or too expensive for smallholder farmers to obtain. As a result, many smallholders already use natural, low-input, pesticide-free methods, and have done so for generations but aren't able to command the higher prices demanded by the organic certification label. This doesn't mean you shouldn't buy organically certified coffee, but it does mean you shouldn't buy organic coffee *exclusively*.

When it comes to fair trade, a similar story plays out. Farms that obtain fair trade certification are prohibited from using child or forced labor, and in return, fair trade sets a minimum price which ensures more stability and better prices for coffee farmers. This helps to minimize the risk of volatile commodity pricing, and also helps small coffee producers to obtain market access under decent conditions.

However, some observers believe that global certification systems represent a form of neocolonialism. Sociologists Cole and Brown argue in their 2014 paper *The Problem with Fair Trade Coffee* that "embedding the regulation of labor rights in a transnational market" can undermine in-country labor organizing efforts.

Others argue that guaranteeing prices doesn't provide a quality incentive to farmers. It is thought that farmers may reserve their higher-quality coffee for a better price on the open market, while selling the other, lower quality coffee, for a guaranteed minimum price through fair trade. Conversely, some farmers use the extra money to invest in their farms, enabling them to produce better-quality coffee all round.

As far as wide-ranging ethical solutions go, there aren't a whole lot of options available to your everyday coffee consumer, and there is no argument that fair trade can make an immense difference to individual farmers. However, there simply is not enough demand for fair-trade coffee. Only 20 percent of the coffee produced to fair-trade standards can be sold as fair trade. The rest ends up being sold for lower prices on the regular market anyway.

A common alternative is a direct-trade model, which aims to shorten the supply chain and increase transparency. It is often employed within specialty coffee, but is it a good solution? Many specialty exporters, trading companies, and even roasters try to support farmers to reach a quality threshold through farm and education advancement initiatives. However, direct trade brings about its own set of issues, given the politicization of coffee trade—it's become a catch-all marketing term for quality-driven, ethically supplied coffee, and there's no independent body ensuring that coffee transactions meet any set standards. Many coffee companies publish their own ethical standards on their websites instead.

As you can see, there's no perfect solution. The best you can do is be an educated consumer: research your beans and the roaster, and try to find an option that you feel good about.

What You'll Need

Measuring cups and spoons

Note that standard sizes differ around the world—the following recipes were developed with U.S measures, but using others will usually not make a big difference.

Scales

Try to find electric scales with a metric setting, that are accurate to 0.1 of a gram.

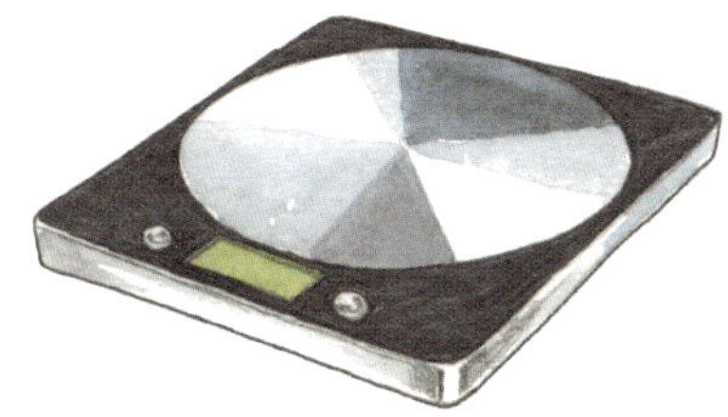

Coffee beans

Whole beans of good quality, from your preferred origin and roast level. Some recipes call for a specific roast level to achieve the closest to the traditional flavor.

Coffee grinder

Preferably a high-quality burr grinder. (See Grinding Coffee page 14)

Coffee brewer

You can use your regular coffee brewing equipment if you can't find or don't want to buy the specific equipment listed in each recipe. However, make sure that you are brewing an equivalent strength coffee. For example, you can use a French press or a filter coffee maker interchangeably, but you'll need to dilute espresso or an espresso capsule to achieve the same strength. (See Brewing Coffee page 16)

Fine mesh sieve

Many recipes are brewed in a saucepan or large pot, and will need to be filtered. You could also use a piece of cheesecloth or a coffee filter.

Gooseneck kettle

For many of the recipes, you will need to pour hot water in a slow and steady stream. Baristas use a gooseneck kettle to control the water flow accurately.

COFFEE AROUND THE WORLD

Entire books could be written on the etymology of coffee, but it is usually traced back to the Turkish *kahve* and the Arabic *qahwa* (believed to be an ancient term for wine). Historical texts began to appear across Europe in the sixteenth century as travelers and merchants encountered this intriguing drink abroad. They attempted phonetic spellings of its foreign name, and as they introduced the drink to the rest of the world, the name continued to be adapted—but never strayed too far from its roots.

ቡና Buna
Amharic

Cà phê
Vietnamese

Café
Spanish
French
Portuguese

Caffè
Italian

Cafea
Romanian

Caife
Irish

Coffi
Welsh

Gáffe
Northern Sámi

Ikhofi
Zulu

ກາເຟ Ka fe
Lao

Kaapi
India

กาแฟ Kāfæ
Thai

Kafe
Haitian Creole

Kafeega
Somali

Kafè
Maltese

קפה Kafeh
Hebrew

Kafea
Basque

Καφές Kafés
Greek

Kaffe
Swedish
Norwegian
Danish

Kaffee
German

咖啡 Kāfēi
Chinese

Kaffi
Icelandic

Kahawa
Swahili

Kahve
Turkish

កាហ្វេ Kahve
Khmer

Kahvia
Finnish

Kape
Filipino

कफी Kaphī
Nepali

ਕਾਫੀ Kāphī
Punjabi

காப்பி Kāppi
Tamil

Kas fes
Hmong

Káva
Slovak

Kava
Croatian

קאַווע Kave
Yiddish

Kavos
Lithuanian

Kawa
Polish

Kawhe
Māori

ᎧᏫ Kawi
Cherokee

ကော်ဖီ Kawhpe
Burmese

커피 Keopi
Korean

Кофе
Russian
Mongolian

Kofe
Samoan
Uzbek

कॉफ़ी Kofee
Hindi

Koffie
Dutch
Afrikaans

コーヒー Kōhī
Japanese

Kohvi
Estonian

Kope
Hawaiian

કોફી Kōphī
Gujarati

Kopi
Malay
Indonesian

قهوة Qahwa
Arabic

Qehwe
Kurdish

The Plant That Changed the World

Coffee's journey began in East Africa, where it was originally consumed as food; and in the Arabian Peninsula, where it was first made into a drink.

Given that our infatuation with coffee spans many centuries and continents, it is no wonder that we encounter great difficulty extracting facts from legend when something as romanticized as coffee is concerned.

There are many origin myths describing where and when our paths first crossed. These days, the most common legend is of Khaldi, a young Ethiopian goatherd who found his goats filled with energy after chewing on an unusual plant. After trying it himself and feeling energized, he brought some back to the monastery where he lived, where it was disapproved of and thrown into the fire. The roasting coffee emitted that intoxicating smell we all know and love, and the rest was history.

There are many variants of this origin story—some begin in Yemen, some in Ethiopia, some were goatherds, some were Sufi mystics or dervishes. What we do know for certain is that two of the most important *Coffea* species, *arabica* and *canephora (robusta)*, originated in the forests of Ethiopia and South Sudan. Here, it is likely coffee was firstly consumed as a foodstuff: ground and rolled into balls with fat, the cherries cooked in butter, or the twigs and leaves infused into milk or tea.

Although cultivation of the coffee plant was largely spread around the world by European colonialists and missionaries, the roots of the drink are Islamic. Early Arabic traders brought roasted coffee with them to drink and trade as they traveled. Some of the earliest known records of coffee being consumed as a beverage are generally accepted to be by Sufi Muslim religious orders in the fifteenth century. However, there are records of what is assumed to be coffee serving pottery from Turkey, Egypt, and Persia by 1350; and a recent archaeological dig in the United Arab Emirates unearthed a single roasted coffee bean thought to be from the twelfth century.

Regardless of the exact date we began to drink coffee, coffee and the coffeehouse quickly spread throughout the Arab world. From there, global exploration, colonialism, and trade brought the powerful coffee bean to many different cultures: where it irreversibly changed (for better or worse) societies, ecosystems, both cultural and physical landscapes, and lives.

Coffee cherries grow in clusters on shrubs and small trees, having developed from fragrant white blossoms. Initially green, the cherries ripen through orange to a deep red color when ready for harvesting.

COFFEE CULTIVATION AND PLANTING

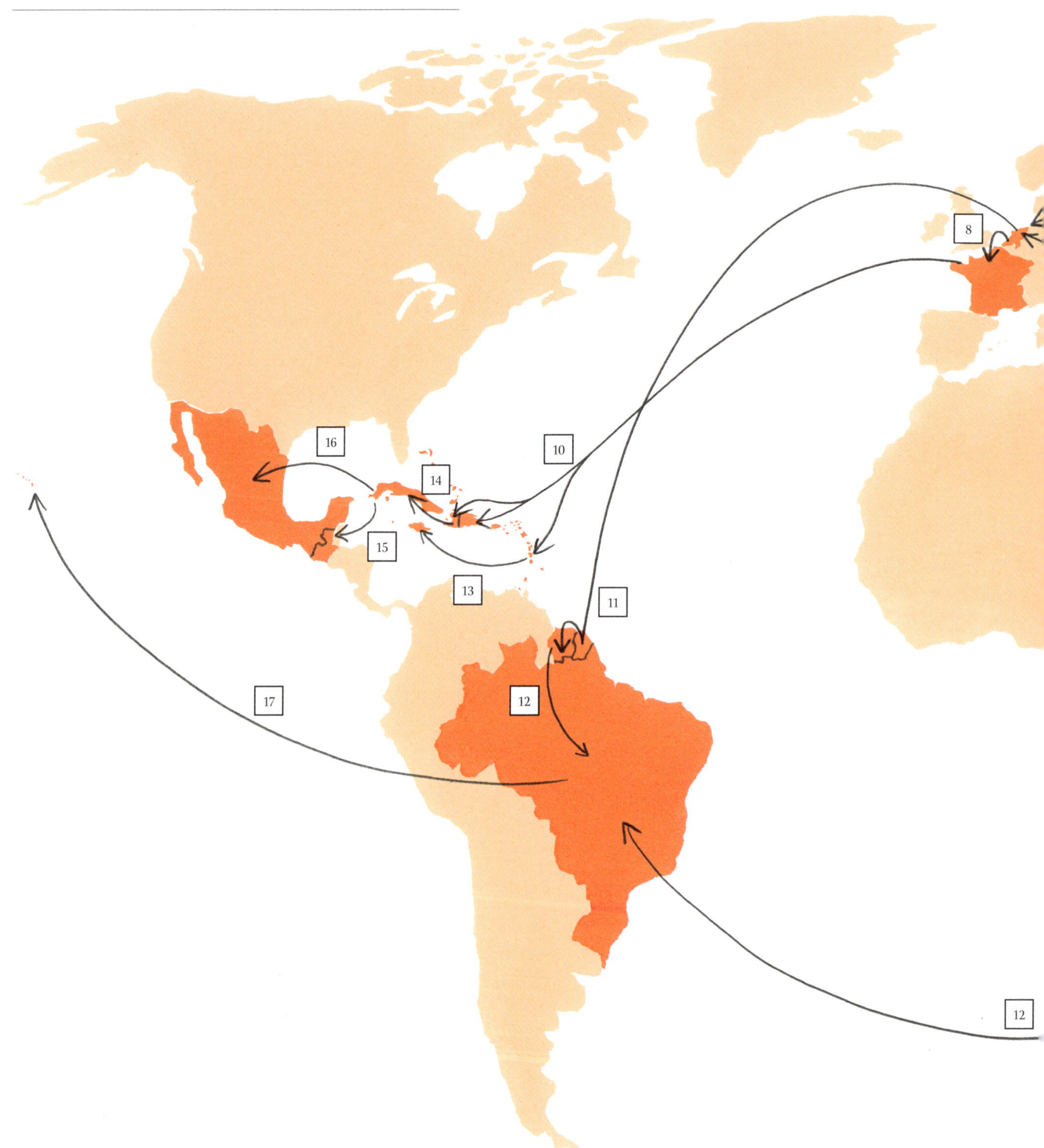

[1] Native to *Ethiopia* and *South Sudan*, used for time immemorial across Africa

[2] By the 1400s *Ethiopia → Yemen*

[3] Early 1500s *Yemen → Sri Lanka* by the Arabs and mid-1600s by the Dutch

[4] By the 1600s *Yemen → India* by Indian Sufi Saint Baba Budan and late 1600s by the Dutch

[5] Early 1600s *Yemen → The Netherlands* by the Dutch

[6] Late 1600s *Yemen → India → Java* (Indonesia) by the Dutch

[7] Early 1700s *Java* (Indonesia) *→ The Netherlands* by the Dutch

[8] Early 1700s *The Netherlands → France* by the Dutch

[9] Early 1700s *Yemen → Réunion Island* by the French

[10] Early 1700s *France → The Caribbean* (the islands of Martinique and Hispaniola, now Haiti and Dominican Republic) by the French

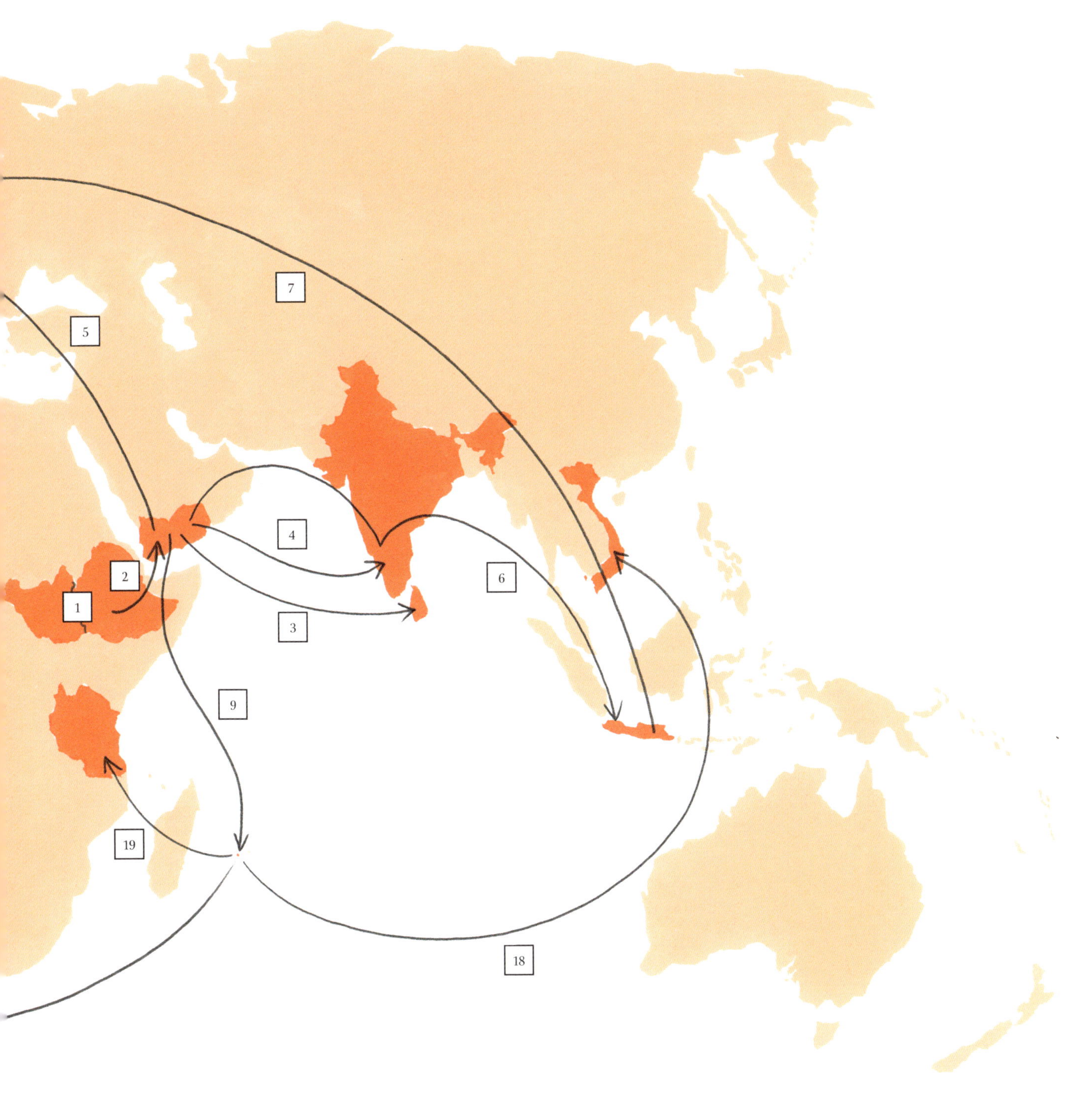

[11] Early 1700s
The Netherlands → Suriname
by the Dutch
→ French Guiana

[12] Early 1700s
French Guiana → Brazil
by the Portuguese
and mid-1800s from
Réunion Island (Bourbon)

[13] Mid-1700s
Martinique → Jamaica
by the British

[14] Mid-1700s
Santo Domingo
(now Dominican
Republic) *→ Cuba*
by the Spanish

[15] Mid-1700s
The Caribbean
(Cuba or Antilles)
→ Guatemala
by the Spanish

[16] Late 1700s
The Caribbean (Cuba)
→ Mexico
by the Spanish

[17] Early 1800s
Brazil → Hawai'i
by the Chief of O'ahu

[18] Mid-1800s
Réunion Island → Vietnam
by the French

[19] Late 1800s
Réunion Island → Tanzania
by the French, *Arabica*
cultivation

Home of Espresso, the World-Changing Coffee

1906, Milan: the world was introduced to the first *caffè espresso* when business partners Pavoni and Bezzera presented their pressure-brewing machines at a convention. These were the forerunners of all modern espresso machines.

Italy is the home of the espresso—a small coffee drink that has had a huge worldwide influence. *Un caffè* (espresso), is the concentrated extraction of coffee produced by the espresso machine and is the base of hundreds of coffee-based beverages. Italy's centuries-long national romance with coffee has not abated: today, around 150,000 coffee bars make espresso across the country, and surveys suggest that 90 percent of Italian adults have drunk coffee in the last 24 hours.

By the late sixteenth century, news of coffee had begun to spread beyond the Ottoman Empire, as several physicians, botanists, and travelers wrote of a drink they had encountered in Turkey and Egypt. Although the date of coffee's arrival in Europe is not entirely clear, it is generally assumed the Venetians were the first to encounter it, given their trading connections with, and proximity to Turkey (Greece and some other contemporary European states were part of the Ottoman Empire at the time). A botanical description was published in Italy in 1592, and popular legend (albeit apocryphal) has it that Pope Clement VIII (1536–1605) blessed the Islamic brew, permitting its use by Christians, thus enabling its spread through Italy.

Regardless of the authenticity of this story, coffee did catch on in Italy fairly quickly, with the first *caffetteria* (coffeehouse) opening in Venice in the mid-1600s. The coffeehouses of Turkey and the Arabian Peninsula were thus adopted and adapted into the West. These hubs of socialization, merriment, and liberalization spread across other European countries in quick succession. In Italy today, espressos are regularly drunk *al banco* (at the counter), sometimes with a sweet pastry, in a ritual that may be repeated several times a day.

In 1819, *la cuccuma*, a reversible drip filter coffee pot, was invented by a French tinsmith. This invention enabled even the less affluent, who could not afford to frequent cafés, to prepare and drink good coffee at home. While it is called *la cuccuma* in Naples, this style of coffee maker earned the name *la caffettiera napoletana* (Neapolitan coffee maker) outside of the city. It remained popular across Italy until the invention of the *moka* coffee maker in 1933.

The *moka* ended up being a quicker and easier stovetop coffee maker, using pressure to force hot water through the coffee. It wasn't long before it became the most-popular at-home method in Italy. It can now be found from the Dominican Republic to Australia, and goes by many names: *caffettiera*, *greca*, *cafetera*, *macchinetta*, or *la cafetera italiana*. The *moka* uses pressure to brew, so it is often called a stovetop espresso maker—but because the pressure is lower than that of an espresso machine, the *caffè della moka* (*moka* coffee) is not considered true espresso.

CORRIERE DELLA SERA
VENERDÌ 24 GENNAIO 2020
GRAND HOTEL VESUVIO NAPOLI
SCARPA
Consensi e società
LE ALTRE FACCE DELL'EMILIA
di Dario Di Vico
La pragmatica von der Leyen incassa la tregua sui dazi Usa
NAPOLI

20
19

The espresso machine was an invention of convenience. Before its introduction, coffee took up to five minutes to brew. As the number of cafés across Europe grew, inventors saw an opportunity to create a commercial machine that would help speed up the process. The nineteenth century was the age of steam, so it made sense to use steam pressure to brew coffee.

The invention of espresso was a product of its time; patents and inventions for similar technology were cropping up all over Europe, around the same time. The first step is usually credited to a man named Angelo Moriondo, from Piedmont, Italy, who registered a patent for a steam-powered brewer in the late 1800s, although it doesn't appear his machines were produced commercially.

Many Italian espresso coffee blends, though largely *arabica,* blend in a little *robusta* to help create an excellent *crema*—considered a necessity for proper espresso.

Then, in 1901, Luigi Bezzera obtained a patent for his own coffee machine. Bezzera worked with a business colleague, Desiderio Pavoni, to produce and improve the machine; they introduced the world to the modern *caffè espresso* at the Milan International, a world fair, in 1906. These were the first machines to brew a single cup at a time, and it is said they did so in around 45 seconds.

Technology advanced, and other manufacturers and inventors continued to innovate until a practical method was developed and manufactured by Achille Gaggia in 1946. This machine was originally hand powered and was the first to produce a *crema,* the flavorful foam that sits atop a good espresso. Eventually, this machine evolved into the modern, electric-powered espresso machine we know today. Many Italian espresso coffee blends, though largely *arabica,* blend in a little *robusta* to help create an excellent *crema*—considered a necessity for proper espresso.

It was not long before these Italian machines were exported around the world, putting espresso-based beverages into the hands of consumers from London to Beijing. The large-scale emigration of Italians after the Second World War helped proliferate Italian coffee culture: wherever Italians went, espresso machines were imported shortly after. Coffee had been consumed in many of these countries for hundreds of years, but the brews were often a far cry from the hand-pulled espressos the Italians were used to.

The 1950s and 1960s became the era of espresso, from the United Kingdom to Australia. In London, Italians helped to revive the bomb-damaged area of Soho by building vibrant cafés. Appalled at what passed for coffee at the time, they set about bringing in the machinery, coffee beans, and coffee styles, while establishing the friendly neighborhood cafés worthy of their homeland.

You'll find coffee culture varies across Italy, too: in Turin, chocolate and coffee perfectly combine in the *bicerin,* in which hot chocolate, coffee, and whipped cream or milk are layered in a short glass.

Although many espresso-based drinks outside of Italy have retained Italian names, often, these words don't always match with what you'd find in the cup in Italy. In Italian, *latte,* for example, simply means milk. So unless you'd like a cold glass of milk, you'd need to →

→ order a *caffè latte* (coffee and milk). The *piccolo latte* (small latte, a ristretto topped with a small amount of steamed milk) has an Italian name, but it's actually thought to have been invented in Australia. What you can find in Italy is the *caffè macchiato,* an espresso with a dollop of milk foam. If you are looking for a milk-heavy coffee, the *cappuccino* is traditionally one-third espresso, one-third steamed milk, and one-third foam (and should never be ordered after midday because it is considered a breakfast item). *Caffè con panna* adds a dollop of cream to the top of your espresso, while *caffè corretto* (corrected coffee) is a shot of espresso with a few drops of grappa, sambuca, or brandy.

> Wherever Italians went, espresso machines were imported shortly after. Coffee had been consumed in many of these countries for hundreds of years, but the brews were often a far cry from the hand-pulled espressos the Italians were used to.

An espresso shot can be brewed *ristretto* (restricted), *normale* (normal), or *lungo* (long), where more or less water is extracted through the same amount of coffee. Although the coffee weight is the same, the beans are ground differently, so the flow rate can be controlled to ensure the coffee is not over- or under-extracted. The staple Italian restaurant dessert, *affogato al caffè* (drowned in coffee), is a hot espresso shot poured over cold, sweet vanilla ice cream or *fior di latte* gelato, and is beloved worldwide.

You'll find coffee culture varies across Italy, too: in Turin, chocolate and coffee perfectly combine in the *bicerin,* in which hot chocolate, coffee, and whipped cream or milk are layered in a short glass. For the *caffè marocchino,* invented in another Piedmont town, Alessandria, a layer of cocoa powder is added to the espresso, then topped with another layer of foamed milk. The chocolate and hazelnut paste *gianduja* was invented in Turin, and in drinks across the Piedmont region, you can sometimes find *gianduja* used instead of chocolate.

There are dozens of other recent additions to Italian *caffetteria* menus, too, such as the *caffè al ginseng,* a blend of coffee and ginseng popularized in Asia and now a hit in Italy, too. Or, the *caffè shakerato,* in which espresso and ice cubes are blended in a cocktail shaker with simple syrup and served in a martini glass.

Italian coffee culture goes beyond the beans, the equipment, and the place in which it is consumed. Traditions and culture run deep and vary across the country. In many coffee bars, you'll need to find the cash register first, pay for your drink, and then you may order from the *baristi* by waving your paper receipt to catch their attention among the throng of other patrons.

Caffè sospeso (suspended coffee) is a charitable tradition that began in Naples in the late 1800s: a customer pays for two coffees, drinks one, and leaves the other as an anonymous act of charity. A later customer can then ask about a *caffè sospeso* and be served one for free.

From Caffè Florian in Venice to Caffè Gilli in Florence and Gran Caffè Gambrinus in Naples (opposite and previous page), Italy's historic coffeehouses continue to practice long-established traditions in rooms with exquisite interiors.

FLORIAN
CAFFE

Gambrinus
NAPOLI
Shop on line

Caffè Espresso

Espresso Coffee

Invented in Italy around the turn of the twentieth century, the espresso machine has heavily influenced coffee culture worldwide ever since. In Italy, espresso still rules: 93 percent of all coffee drunk there is prepared as espresso. This concentrated, flavorful, and aromatic coffee results from hot water being forced under pressure through finely ground coffee beans in an espresso machine.

Water

7 g coffee
Grind size: fine

You will also need:
Espresso machine, scales, timer

Let water run through the espresso machine without the portafilter attached to flush out any old coffee grounds. Insert a single 7 g filter basket into the portafilter.

Measure out the coffee into the basket using a scale.

Level out the bed of coffee. Water follows the path of least resistance, so if the grounds are distributed unevenly, the water will flow unevenly, which will affect the flavor.

Rest the portafilter on the counter, and hold the tamper with the top in the palm of your hand. Place your thumb and forefinger on opposing sides of the base of the tamper, and place into the portafilter basket. Using your thumb and forefinger—now touching the edges of both the basket and the tamper—make sure the tamper is sitting straight and level. Press down hard. Put the portafilter into the espresso machine and pull it tight. Place a serving cup on a set of scales underneath and tare to zero. Start extraction and press start on a timer.

As the coffee extracts, keep an eye on both the weight and the time. For a standard Italian 1:3 brew ratio, 7 g of coffee in should weigh around 21 g in the cup. For light to medium roasts, or a third-wave style extraction, try an 18 g double shot (using a double-shot sized filter basket), which should result in 36 g of coffee in the cup. Either of these should extract within 20–35 seconds.

Coffee grind size is very important to get right. The correct flow rate will keep the shot from over- or under-extracting. If you yield too much coffee in the cup within the time frame, grind the beans finer, which will slow down extraction. If you yield too little, the grind needs to be coarser, which will speed up extraction.

If you are brewing in an environment with changing humidity levels (such as a kitchen, or if you often open your window), you may find that a grind size that works one day may not work the next. This is because coffee is hygroscopic and will absorb moisture from the air. For that reason, a more humid day could cause the ground coffee to swell, which in turn, results in a tighter packed portafilter—and a slower extraction. In most professional environments, the coffee grind is adjusted throughout the day according to the environment and flow rate.

At home, if you consistently use scales and a timer to extract, you will quickly gain an understanding of what a perfectly extracted espresso looks and tastes like. Then, you can begin to make adjustments in grind size to cater to the environment, coffee bean type, or even your taste preference.

Notes:

Coffee brewing is very much down to personal preference, although it's good to note that darker roasts shine with shorter brew times (the longer roast makes the bean less dense and more soluble), and lighter roasts with longer brew times. Any type of roast may be used—in Italy darker roasts are preferred, while American coffee producers often tend towards much lighter roasts. A traditional Italian brew ratio of 1:3 is considered a *normale* espresso in Italy. However, if you prefer lightly roasted coffee or the espresso found in many specialty coffee shops, I encourage you to use closer to a 1:1.5–1:2 brew ratio. For more information, see "about brew ratios" on page 17.

Caffè con la moka

Coffee Made with the *moka* Pot

Using the affordable stovetop espresso maker, known as the *macchinetta, moka* pot, *greca,* or *cafetera* is a simple way to brew something close to a *caffè espresso* at home. It is a very common way of preparing coffee in Italy, Spain, France, and Latin America.

Water

Coffee
Grind size: medium fine

You will also need:
Stovetop espresso maker

Take apart your stovetop espresso maker. Fill the bottom chamber with water up to below the steam release valve.

Insert the funnel filter, making sure the water, with the insert in place, still does not cover the steam release valve. The coffee should be ground a little finer than for drip coffee, slightly coarser than for espresso. Fill the funnel with ground coffee—do not compress. Tap the funnel gently to even out the grounds.

Without tamping, run a finger around the edge of the filter to make sure there are no stray grounds (this will ensure a tight seal), and then tightly screw on the top half of the stovetop espresso maker.

Place it on the stove over medium heat. If using gas, the flame should cover the bottom of the pot but not heat the handle.

After a few minutes, you will hear the pot begin to gurgle. About 15 seconds after you first hear this sound, remove it from the heat. It should continue to percolate until the top chamber is full.

Notes:
You can buy *moka* pots in 2, 4, 6, or more cups. Each manufacturer will recommend different volumes of water and coffee. Consult the manual for your specific pot if you need further guidance. Be aware that the stovetop espresso maker can be very similar in looks to the stovetop percolator, but very, very different in the way it works. With stovetop espresso, the water is forced through the grinds at pressure and collects in the top. A percolator will continually run water through the grinds until it is removed from the heat.

BIALETTI

Bicerin

Espresso with Hot Chocolate and Cream

According to local lore, in eighteenth-century Turin, Italy, a local coffeehouse made their own version of the *bavareisa,* a chocolate, coffee, and milk beverage fashionable at the time. Named the *bicerin,* meaning small glass, this layered sweet beverage is usually drunk before noon and is now popular all across the Piedmont region.

¼ cup heavy cream

1 tsp powdered sugar

¼ cup milk

40 g (1 ½ oz) dark chocolate, chopped

1 double espresso, or 60 ml (2 fl oz) strong black coffee

Cocoa powder, for dusting

Whip the cream with the powdered sugar in a bowl until it forms stiff peaks.

Heat the milk in a small saucepan, adding the chopped chocolate as it starts to warm. Stir until the milk is hot and the chocolate melts, but do not let it boil. Keep it at just below a simmer and continue stirring until the mixture thickens a little.

Pour the hot chocolate mixture into a serving glass, then gently pour in the espresso, over the back of a spoon, to preserve the layers. Spoon the cream on top and dust with cocoa powder.

Notes:

The *bicerin* has many regional variations. In Piedmont, the home of *gianduja* (a rich chocolate and hazelnut paste) you can sometimes find a little blended into this drink. Elsewhere, the *bicerin* falls out of favor and is replaced by the *caffè marocchino,* a similar drink but with an extra layer of cocoa powder added to the top of the espresso, upon which another layer of foamed milk is added.

Coffee Culture and Ceremony in Ethiopia

Over the past millennium, Ethiopia: ancestors of the Oromo people have ground coffee cherries, mixed them with fat, and rolled the mixture into large balls, sometimes surviving only on this sustenance during long journeys.

Although we don't know exactly when coffee was discovered, we do know that the two most important *Coffea* species, *arabica* and *canephora (robusta)*, originated in the forests of Ethiopia and South Sudan. There are an estimated 6,000–15,000 heirloom varieties of coffee in Ethiopia, many growing wild, and have yet to be discovered.

Coffee has been consumed in social settings or gatherings such as peace-making meetings for centuries, and the ritual of coffee consumption is of key importance to relations between ethnic groups and societies. Anthropologist Éloi Ficquet, a contributor to the book *Ethiopia: History, Culture and Challenges*, writes that the Oromo people (who currently represent around one-third of Ethiopia's population) hold rich oral traditions and symbols that support a coffee culture that spans centuries. The Oromo say that the first coffee plant grew from the tears of *Waaqa* (God). The plant was, and still is, used in ceremonies to honor *Waaqa*. Other ethnic groups hold their own varied oral traditions surrounding coffee's origins, too numerous to detail here—but what can be said is that the art of coffee-making is central to Ethiopian culture.

Scholars believe that the ancestors of the Oromo people and their neighboring societies (such as the Hadiya, the Dawro, or Kafa) may have been the first to consume coffee as a foodstuff. While local oral histories predate most written records, detailed observances of consumption practices by European travelers began around the seventeenth and eighteenth centuries. Scottish travel writer James Bruce wrote about his journeys to Ethiopia, undertaken between 1768–1773, in *Travels to Discover the Source of the Nile*. He observed that the Oromo people—"a wandering nation"—pulverized coffee cherries and mixed them with fat. They formed the mixture into "billiard ball" sized rounds, stored them in leather pouches, and ate only these for energy during long journeys.

Ficquet also documents a variety of traditional regional recipes found throughout Ethiopia: "a paste of butter mixed with crushed berries (ripe or roasted); infusions of the leaves, barks, or twigs of the coffee tree in milk; whole berries cooked in butter." Various preparations of coffee are also prevalent in traditional medicine. Wine is also made, either from the fruit and skin or the coffee beans themselves. The coffee leaf, griddled or sun-dried, is pounded and made into a tea called *kuti*. But perhaps the most important aspect of coffee in Ethiopian culture is the coffee ceremony.

Practiced across Ethiopia and Eritrea, in all types of households, the coffee ceremony is a key element of a unified national identity across more than 80 ethnic groups. *Buna dabo naw* (coffee is bread) is a commonly used phrase that perfectly exemplifies the importance coffee has in Ethiopian life.

While the ritual varies slightly regionally, ቡና *buna* (coffee) is consumed daily and prepared ceremonially. Grass or straw is laid out on the floor, which is sometimes decorated with flowers. Smoke, like a →

→ phantom dancing cobra, rises from burning frankincense and hot charcoal. Some people refuse to drink coffee unless frankincense has first been burned because it is said to get rid of negative energy.

A metal roasting pan is placed over the hot coals, and more intense smoke—from coffee roasting—joins the fragrant incense. A woman is always in charge of preparing the coffee: it's a well-practiced routine.

In all types of households, the coffee ceremony is a key element of a unified national identity across more than 80 ethnic groups.

The beans pop and crackle, turning a dark brown, and are roasted past the second crack. It is traditionally a very dark roast, but brewing the coffee with sugar and various aromatic additions balances the intensity. Sugar is relatively new to the coffee ceremony because it was a rare commodity in Ethiopia before the 1970s. Before then, and still in some places today, salt was used.

The pure *arabica* beans, once roasted, are ground coarsely while still hot. A ሙቀጫ *muk'echa* and ዘነዘና *zenezena* (mortar and pestle) are used to pound the beans. The clay ጀበና *jebena* (brewing pot) is filled with water and brought to a boil, and the coffee is added slowly. As the brew boils up into the top of the thin-necked brewing pot, the hostess deftly tips a little into a small jug and then pours it back into the pot, regulating the temperature. Practice and tradition tell her when the brew is ready: she will judge by the color and smell.

Balled-up horsehair or other similar material are traditionally used as a filter, pushed into the neck of the *jebena*. Sometimes a bundle of saffron is used instead, adding a floral note. Different spices may be added before brewing, such as cardamom, cloves, cinnamon, or fresh ginger. A twig of ጤና አዳም *Tena'Adam* (rue, a perennial herb that has been used medicinally for centuries) is sometimes served alongside the coffee for stirring. The oils that are extracted from the rue have a fig- or citrus-like flavor. In some places, ንጥር ቅቤ *niter qibe* (spiced, clarified butter) is added.

When the coffee is ready, it is poured into a ስኒ *sïni* (small, handleless cup about the size of a *demitasse*) from a height of about one foot. The *sïni* sits on a low table, the ረከቦት *rekebot,* considered the altar of the ceremony. The coffee is served first to the oldest person in the group, or the most distinguished guest. The pot is refilled with water and returned to the fire. The first round of coffee brewing is called አቦል *abol,* which means first; the second brewing is called ቶና *tona* (second); and the third, በረካ *baraka,* means blessing. The Arabic roots of these words indicate strong long-term connections between the coffee cultures of Ethiopia and Yemen.

Another integral part of coffee drinking in Ethiopia is the snacks that accompany coffee: ቆሎ *kolo* (roasted grains such as barley), ዳቦ *dabo* (spiced honey wheat bread), እንጀራ *injera* (a fermented pancake made from teff flour that is eaten throughout Ethiopia and Eritrea), or popped grains such as sorghum, an earthy, nutty grain that has been cultivated in Africa for more than 4,000 years. An offer to join someone for coffee is a show of respect or friendship: a welcome prepared for any guest, at any time of day.

Coffee drinking remains a hallmark of Ethiopian hospitality. It serves as an important social ritual and is a time for sharing with neighbors, friends, and relatives rather than drinking alone.

ቡና Buna

SERVES 1

Coffee

Buna is prepared during a detailed coffee ceremony in Ethiopia, using many pieces of unique brewing equipment. It is an everyday ritual, and frankincense is often burned while the coffee is roasted dark over a fire by hand. Brewed in an Ethiopian clay coffee pot called a *jebena*, it is then served, sweetened, and the pot returned to the fire for repeated rounds.

¼ cup green coffee beans per serving

1 cup water per serving

Optional, per serving:
2 pods korarima *(Ethiopian black cardamom) or Indian black cardamom, 2–3 cloves, 1 cinnamon stick, pinch of saffron, 1 tsp ground ginger, 1 rue leaf or rue twig*

Sugar, to taste

Popcorn, for serving

You will also need:
Small wok or pan, woven natural fiber mat, jebena *(Ethiopian clay coffee pot),* sini *(cups), or demitasse cups*

Rinse the coffee beans and pat dry, removing and discarding any beans that look defective.

Place the coffee beans in a small wok or pan, then set over a medium heat. Continuously shake the pan from side to side as the beans roast to ensure they are roasted evenly. They will begin to darken, and once they begin to smoke (when they are uniformly dark brown or black), remove the pan from the heat and carefully wave the pan around the room, to allow the guests to smell the aroma of the roasted coffee.

Carefully pour the beans onto a woven straw or other heatproof natural fiber mat, and, folding the mat a bit so they don't spill, shake the beans a little to help them cool.

Add the water to the *jebena*. If you are using any of the spices, add them to the *jebena* too (except for the saffron, if using). Place over a low heat to bring the water temperature up to just below a simmer.

Once the coffee beans are cool enough to handle, pour them into a grinder and grind medium-fine.

Pour the ground coffee back onto the mat, and then, folding the mat to create a sort of funnel, tip the coffee into the neck of the *jebena*. Swirl the *jebena* to mix the ground coffee through the water.

Bring to a low boil over a low flame. If you have a small *jebena*, or are filling a larger *jebena* at least two-thirds full with water, the coffee will foam up the neck of the *jebena*. Remove from the heat as it rises to control the foam, or, turn the heat down. You might need to carefully tip a little of the liquid into a small pitcher to prevent it from spilling over, then return the *jebena* to the heat →

→ as the foam subsides. You can then pour the coffee from the pitcher back into the *jebena,* too.

If you are using a small volume of water and/or a large *jebena,* you'll need to be careful not to over boil because if the *jebena* isn't at least two-thirds full, you won't get the foam indicating when to turn the heat down.

After the foam rises and subsides a couple of times, remove the *jebena* from the heat. If you are using saffron, add it to the *jebena* now. Leave it to sit for a few minutes as the grinds settle.

If you are using sugar, add it to the cups. Pour the coffee carefully into small cups to serve. Traditionally, the same *buna* is rebrewed multiple times over a drinking session. The first cup is very strong, and they become weaker with each additional brew.

Serve with popcorn or other popped grains.

Notes:

Sometimes, *Tena'Adam* (rue) is used to flavor the coffee. A few leaves are added to the pot, or a rue twig is served with each cup to stir the sugar through, adding flavor as it is stirred. Consume rue at your own risk because it can be toxic in large doses. Others add a pinch of salt, or a bit of *niter qibe*, a spiced, clarified butter. You'll need a *jebena* to brew this version; the success of this recipe is dependent upon the clay pot and its signature shape.

Buna qalaa

CUPS 1.5

Coffee Cooked in Spiced Butter

Buna qalaa, which means slaughtered coffee, is a culturally important coffee meal to the Oromo people and is prepared by cooking coffee cherries in butter. While this important cultural ritual cannot be respectfully adapted into a short recipe, some households and restaurants around Ethiopia also prepare coffee beans in butter as a snack. These are sometimes blended with barley, sugar, butter, or *niter qibe,* a traditional Ethiopian spiced and clarified butter.

1 cup green coffee beans

For the niter qibe:

1 tsp fenugreek seeds

½ tsp ground korarima *(Ethiopian black cardamom)*

¼ tsp ground nutmeg

1 cup butter

½ small onion, chopped

1 tbsp finely chopped garlic

2 tbsp crushed besobela *(Ethiopian basil)*

2 tbsp crushed koseret *(Ethiopian herb related to Mexican oregano)*

To make the niter qibe:

Toast the fenugreek seeds, *korarima,* and nutmeg in a small saucepan or dutch oven until fragrant. Add the butter and, as it melts, add the onion and garlic. Crush the *besobela* and *koseret* leaves between your palms, sprinkle over the butter.

Bring to a simmer, and depending on your butter, you might see a white foam float to the surface. Carefully scoop this off and discard, taking care not to remove any of the spices with it. Alternatively, you can use ghee or other clarified butter and skip this clarification process.

Continue to simmer for 45 minutes. You'll need to make sure to remove and discard any white foam or milk solids from the surface so that they don't burn. Be very careful because the simmering butter will be very hot. If it is boiling rapidly and splashing, turn the heat down until it is at a low simmer.

At the end of the cooking time, turn off the heat, and leave aside to cool slightly, but don't let it set.

Set a fine-mesh cheesecloth or fine strainer over a bowl, and carefully pour the butter through to catch all of the solids (discard the solids). Pour the clarified butter into a clean, airtight jar. This will keep for weeks in the refrigerator.

To make the buna qalaa:

Rinse the coffee beans and pat dry, removing and discarding any beans that look defective.

Place the coffee beans in a small pan, then set over a medium heat. Continuously shake the pot from side to side as the beans roast to ensure they are roasted evenly. They will begin to darken, and once they begin to smoke (when they are uniformly dark brown or black), remove from the heat.

Over a low heat, gradually stir ¼–½ cup of the spiced butter into the roasted beans, a tablespoon at a time. Keep stirring and add more butter once each addition has been absorbed. Once the coffee stops absorbing butter, remove from heat and leave to cool.

Store in an airtight jar and eat as a snack. Save the rest of the *niter qibe* for your next batch, or use it as a base for many Ethiopian dishes.

Notes:

The listed Ethiopian herbs and spices are necessary to create authentic flavor, but if you aren't able to source these, here are a few possible substitutes. *Korarima* is a local large, black cardamom. You can use Indian black cardamom as a substitute, although it does taste very different. If you can't find *besobela,* Ethiopian basil, you can use *tulsi* (holy basil) instead. There is not really a good substitute for *koseret* (known as the butter clarifying herb), but in a pinch, you could try Mexican oregano. While it has a very, very different flavor, it's at least in the same genus. Add a pinch of lemon verbena too, to replicate *koseret*'s lemony flavor.

From Kilimanjaro to Peaberries in Tanzania

Ancient history, African Great Lakes: the Haya people made *amwani* by boiling coffee cherries with grassy herbs, then smoking and drying them. It is traded, chewed, and used in offerings and social gatherings to this day.

In the East African country of Tanzania, the topography varies widely, from the peaks of Mount Kilimanjaro (the world's highest single free-standing mountain) to Lake Tanganyika (the world's second-deepest lake). Tanzania lies just south of the equator and its coffee has a global reputation for being of high quality, particularly that grown in the fertile volcanic soil surrounding Mount Kilimanjaro.

In 1964, shortly after gaining independence from the British, the independent states of Tanganyika and Zanzibar merged to become the United Republic of Tanzania. Before 1964, these two states had very different histories, especially related to coffee.

Tanganyika, which covered mainland Tanzania, was an area of East Africa partitioned by imperial powers into German East Africa. After the First World War, the region became a British mandate and was renamed Tanganyika Territory. Long before German and British presence, however, overland trade routes that linked the African Great Lakes and the coast wove their way across the country. More than 120 ethnic groups call the geographic and political area now known as Tanzania home, including the Haya and many others for whom coffee has been a central part of their culture for centuries.

Tanzania has become well known for its quality peaberry coffee, particularly in the United States. With peaberry coffee, only one seed develops in the coffee cherry instead of the usual two. Some people incorrectly believe that the peaberry is a variety of coffee grown in Tanzania, a mutation, or that Tanzania produces more of this than other places, but peaberries can occur anywhere, and make up only around 5–10 percent of any given harvest.

Many of the briefer accounts of coffee history, including some official Tanzanian ones, emphasize the story of the introduction of coffee to Tanzania by French Catholic missionaries. While it is true that they brought *Coffea arabica* to the Bagamoyo and subsequently Kilimanjaro regions in the mid-to-late 1800s, it is often misconstrued as the very beginning of Tanzania's relationship with coffee.

This often obscures much of mainland Tanzania's precolonial coffee history. At least 16 wild *Coffea* species have been officially recorded as indigenous. According to A. S. Thomas in his paper *Types of Robusta coffee and their selection in Uganda*, published in *The East African Agricultural Journal* in 1935, both wild and domesticated *Coffea canephora* (*robusta*) were identified in Tanzania well before the colonial era. Haya oral histories also note that *robusta* has been consumed by the Haya and their ancestors since time immemorial.

Perhaps the precolonial story about *robusta* is so often overlooked because *arabica* is now Tanzania's main coffee export; or, perhaps it is that much of the earlier traditional coffee culture relied on access to live coffee plants. The fresh coffee cherry is integral to both ceremonial and everyday traditions. In his book *Sacred Trees, Bitter Harvests*, Brad Weiss notes that →

TAMU

The Art of Aroma Perception in Coffee
E-n-z-y-m-a-t-i-c
Flowery
Fruity
Herbal
Lemon
Tea Rose
Apple
Honeyed
Apricot
Potato
Cucumber
The Art of Aroma Perception in Coffee
S-u-g-a-r B-r-o-w-n-i-n-g
Carmelly
Nutty
Chocolaty
Roasted Hazelnuts
Dark Chocolate
Fresh Butter
Roasted Almonds
Vanilla
Walnuts
Toast

→ *amwani* (Haya coffee) is prepared by boiling unripened coffee cherries, still in their green husks, along with grassy herbs in large pots. The cherries are then smoked and dried over the course of several days. The coffee is then ready to consume—not by extracting into a beverage, but by chewing the cherries whole. Coffee was also consumed in a similar way by other people in East Africa.

Traditional coffee ceremonies in Zanzibar draw influence from Arabic coffee culture. Beans are roasted in clay pots over charcoal and mixed with spices such as vanilla, cardamom, cinnamon, ginger, and lemongrass.

Weiss details several other ways coffee was, and still is, important to Haya society. In a list that is by no means exhaustive, he points out that the coffee cherry was important for rituals, divination practices, currency and trade, societal interaction and relationship-building, and for devotional offerings. Expansion was carefully controlled by kings and nobles, who allowed coffee to proliferate not via seed but by controlled propagated cuttings.

Although comprising less than 0.2 percent of Tanzania's total land area, the Zanzibar archipelago has had more than its fair share of history. Evidence of human occupation on the island began almost 20,000 years ago, but we will jump into the story around the second half of the first millennium.

Here we have evidence of Zanzibar as a key player in the Indian Ocean trade, integral to East-West exchanges throughout history. Although having few natural resources of its own, Zanzibar proved a useful base to make contact and trade with the Swahili coast of eastern Africa, which stretches roughly from Mogadishu, Somalia, in the North to the island of Kilwa in the South. Monsoon winds took traders bearing spices, cloth, beads, and porcelain from Persia, Arabia, and India to the sheltered harbor of Zanzibar, and then when the winds shifted, they returned with ivory, enslaved people, animal skins, spices, and much more. The Omani Sultanate had great influence over Zanzibar, moving the capital from Muscat to Zanzibar in 1840. There was also great interest from Portuguese, German, and British powers in Zanzibar and throughout East Africa. Zanzibar became a British protectorate in 1890, after the British played a part in outlawing the slave trade in the archipelago in the late 1800s.

These imperial powers often pressured mainland Tanganyikan farmers into planting cash crops such as coffee, resulting in the proliferation of *arabica* throughout the land. Mount Kilimanjaro is one of the most productive agricultural regions in Tanzania, and the Chagga people, who predominantly live on homestead plantations on the slopes of Kilimanjaro, have been of key importance in the growing of *arabica* since it was introduced to the region.

Coffee vendors often carry buckets filled with sweets to eat with the black, spiced coffee, such as *kashata*, a popular Swahili sweet made with grated coconut, peanut, or both.

Zanzibar was also a central figure in the spice trade, so much so that it has been referred to as the Spice Islands. Cloves, originally from the Moluccas (Asia's Spice Islands, now part of Indonesia), were grown with great success, along with many other imported spices such as vanilla, pepper, chili, and →

→ nutmeg. Many of these spices found their way into brewed *kahawa* (Swahili for coffee, derived from Arabic *qahwa*). The growth of the spice trade in Zanzibar was not without great expense, however. The Omani sultan encouraged the development of spice plantations, which were almost entirely reliant on slave labor. Just a few years after their genesis, these plantations controlled 90 percent of the world market for cloves—a monopoly that was to continue for the next century.

Traditional coffee ceremonies in Zanzibar draw influence from Arabic coffee culture. Beans are roasted in clay pots over charcoal and mixed with spices such as vanilla, cardamom, cinnamon, ginger, and lemongrass. Today, in Tanzania's port city Dar es Salaam, in Zanzibar, and along the Swahili coast, coffee vendors walk the streets carrying large metal kettles, sometimes adding ginger to the *kikombe* (cup) before pouring the coffee in. The sellers often carry buckets filled with sweets to eat with the black, spiced coffee, such as *kashata*, a popular Swahili sweet made with grated coconut, peanut, or both.

While a more Western form of café culture is gradually taking root in Tanzania's urban centers, vendors with metal kettles continue to take to the streets in the country's coastal towns.

100%
FRANCOPHONE

Kahawa

SERVES 2–3

Spiced Coffee

In Zanzibar and the Swahili coast, coffee culture is influenced by the Arabic coffee of the Omani who used to rule the islands, quality coffee from mainland Tanzania, and an abundance of spice plantations. Coffee spiced with cloves, cinnamon, cardamom, ginger, and lemongrass, is drunk across the islands and the coastal mainland.

2 cups water

3 cardamom pods, lightly crushed

1 small cinnamon stick

1 vanilla bean, split and scraped, or 1 tsp natural vanilla extract

Small piece fresh ginger, sliced

Small piece fresh lemongrass, bruised

3 cloves

5 level tbsp coffee
Grind size: medium

Milk and sugar, to taste (optional)

Bring 2 cups of water to a boil in a pan over high heat. Add the cardamom pods, cinnamon stick, vanilla bean (if using extract, add it later, just before straining, instead), ginger, lemongrass, and cloves. Boil for 10 minutes, covered.

Remove the pan from the heat. Add the ground coffee, and stir through. Cover and leave to infuse for 4 minutes (if using vanilla extract, add it after the 4 minutes are up).

Pour the brew through a fine filter into preheated serving cups. This makes a strong, small coffee to serve 2–3. Add milk and/or sugar to taste, if you like.

Notes:

Packets of coffee can be bought in Zanzibar pre-blended with spices, but locals only use fresh spices. These spices are often added during roasting, but as this recipe calls for already roasted coffee, add the spices during brewing.

A Devotional Drink Conquers the World

1400s, Yemen: Sufi mystics consumed coffee to keep them awake and alert, and to enhance their *dhikr* (religious devotion) during long hours of prayer at nighttime vigils.

Our global infatuation with coffee spans centuries and continents, so it is no wonder that we have difficulty separating fact from legend when trying to ascertain how and when the paths of humans and coffee first crossed. There are a number of origin myths: some begin in Ethiopia, some in Yemen.

What we can state as fact through analysis of genetic markers is that *Coffea arabica* originated somewhere in the forests of what is now Ethiopia, Eritrea and/or South Sudan, and that Yemen had a key part to play in its cultivation and domestication. The hot, dry environment in this southern part of the Arabian Peninsula was very different from the lush forests of Ethiopia, so the coffee trees had to adapt. Those that did so produced flavor profiles that are revered to this day.

The spread of coffee cultivation, brewing, and perhaps even roasting can be credited to Yemeni farmers and to the Sufi mystics who used coffee for devotional purposes. The coffee plant became woven into the cultural and societal fabric of the Islamic world—and, from there, everywhere else.

Author Ralph S. Hattox studied original Arabic texts when researching his book *Coffee and Coffeehouses: The Origins of a Social Beverage in the Medieval Near East.* Hattox points out that early coffee writers, aware of their knowledge gap, found it hard to resist the temptation to supplement their stories with origin myths. As a consequence, many historical accounts contain dramatic inaccuracies, referencing ancient sources that were quoting second- or third-hand eyewitness accounts at best and, at worst, were baseless legend.

Many coffee origin myths have their roots in Yemen. Texts in Arabic and by European travelers to the region tell of various "discoveries," placing coffee's introduction into Yemen anywhere from the sixth century all the way through to the fifteenth. Éloi Ficquet's paper *Many Worlds in a Cup: Identity Transactions in the Legend of Coffee Origins* discusses in detail the narrative transformations these origin myths have gone through, highlighting how "the pleasure of tasting a cup of coffee is heightened by meaningful narrative ingredients that decode and culturally re-encode…"

The first reputable written records of coffee as a beverage date back to the fifteenth century. Brewed by Sufi mystics, قهوة *qahwa* (Arabic for brewed coffee) became an important aid for religious devotion. Opinions differ on who first brought coffee to Yemen, but the people to whom the "discovery" was attributed had usually traveled in Ethiopia. Sufism is not an isolated religious order—many Sufis had regular jobs, too—so it wasn't long before coffee drinking was taken up by the general public. Intoxicating alcohol was prohibited in Muslim society, so it is thought that coffee took its place as a permitted stimulant.

However, recent archaeological evidence supports the theory that coffee was brought to Yemen much earlier. A single coffee bean, dated to around the twelfth century, was found in an archaeological dig site in Ras Al-Khaimah, United Arab Emirates, in the late 1990s. It is thought this coffee was grown in Yemen, so this →

→ discovery may provide evidence of coffee trade and cultivation a few hundred years earlier than was previously thought.

Regardless, Yemen played an instrumental role in coffee's worldwide proliferation. When the Ottoman Empire seized Yemen in 1538, it is likely that coffee, which was growing in popularity at the time, was brought back to Constantinople with the returning conquerors. From there, it is believed to have been introduced to Venetian traders, and the humble bean soon conquered hearts in the West.

> The spread of coffee cultivation, brewing, and perhaps even roasting can be credited to Yemeni farmers and to the Sufi mystics who used coffee for devotional purposes. The coffee plant became woven into the cultural and societal fabric of the Islamic world.

For the next few centuries, Yemen held a monopoly on coffee production. Many report that beans were sterilized before export by lightly boiling, roasting, or by other methods to prevent germination. Others believe that the beans simply lost their germination power after long journeys at sea. As with much of coffee's storied history, various myths detail the demise of Yemen's stronghold: some say it began with the smuggling of viable seeds out of the country by an Indian Sufi; others say it was Dutch cloth merchant Pieter van den Broecke who smuggled a live plant from the Yemeni port of Al-Makha (Mokha).

Free of a preexisting cultural understanding of how coffee should be prepared, the Yemenis did not limit themselves to the roasted coffee bean. Brews were made with unroasted beans, spices were added, or the bean was omitted altogether and the coffee husk (the dried skin of the coffee cherries) was used instead, brewed into a sort of tea. Known as قهوة القشر *qahwat alqishr*, or more commonly, just *qishr* (coffee husk, known elsewhere by its Spanish name, *cascara*), this husk infusion is still widely consumed in Yemen. Both *qishr* and *qahwa* (brewed with coffee beans) are often spiced with ginger, or sometimes cardamom or cinnamon.

Coffee is produced by smallholders who grow a wealth of rare heirloom varieties. They use organic, natural production methods—the same traditional methods that have been employed for centuries. The result is exceptional coffee, although it also often means low yields. Many coffee producers also suffer from water shortages; they are also hampered by a lack of processing infrastructure and, of course, the devastating humanitarian crisis that began in 2015.

Daniele Giovannucci, author of the USAID report *Moving Yemen Coffee Forward*, notes that one of the great difficulties in bringing Yemeni coffee to the world is that there has been no significant, organized effort to characterize the unique coffee varieties present in the country. Many varieties evolved over centuries from ancient *Coffea arabica* stock and are grown nowhere else in the world. When Yemeni coffees do make it into the international market, they are among the most prized, commanding the highest prices at auction.

Much of Yemen's coffee is farmed in medieval highland villages by farmers who have been growing coffee for generations. Beans are often harvested, dried, and aged locally, and the beans are separated from their husks by hand.

قهوة القشر Qishr

Husk Coffee

SERVES 1

Elsewhere considered to be a by-product of coffee production, the coffee fruit, or coffee cherry, holds equal importance to the bean in Yemen. *Qishr* (coffee husks) are brewed into a beverage that is similar to a strong tea, usually sweetened and spiced with ginger, and sometimes with cinnamon or cardamom too.

1 ¼ cup freshly boiled water per serving

20 g (½ cup) qishr *(coffee husks)* (see Notes, below)

½ tsp ground ginger

½ tsp ground cinnamon

Sugar, to taste

Bring the water to a boil. Pulse the *qishr* in a spice grinder or blender 3–4 times, just enough to break up larger pieces.

Transfer the *qishr* to a stovetop kettle or a small pan with a lid, set over a medium heat.

Lightly toast the dry *qishr* until fragrant. Pour the freshly boiled water over the top, then add the ginger and cinnamon. Stir, cover with the lid, turn up the heat to high, and bring to a boil.

Once boiling, remove the lid and turn the heat down low. Leave to simmer for 8–10 minutes.

Remove from the heat and let the *qishr* settle. Pour through a mesh sieve into serving cups. Add sugar and/or dilute with more freshly boiled water to taste.

Notes:

Qishr is known in Latin America as *cascara,* and it has become popular as a drink in other countries in recent years, too. As a part of the coffee plant, *qishr* contains caffeine—although a little less than coffee brewed from the bean. It's fairly easy to find online. Try adding different spices such as a single crushed green cardamom pod or ¼ tsp of caraway seeds per serving. For a quick and easy version, you could also add the water and *qishr* to a French press and leave it to steep—or try it cold brewed!

Ceremony and Generosity in the Arabian Peninsula

1500s onwards, مكة المكرمة Makkah al-Mukarramah (Makkah/Mecca): as coffee drinking spread throughout the Arabian Peninsula, Islamic scholars debated. Is coffee an intoxicant and therefore forbidden under Islamic law?

Coffee spread throughout the Arabian Peninsula quickly, and without hesitation—as it soon would throughout the rest of the world.

From its homeland in Africa, coffee first touched the southernmost tip of the Arabian Peninsula, Yemen (see page 64). According to scholars and local histories, it was brewed by Sufi mystics into قهوة *qahwa* (Arabic for brewed coffee), and it became an important aid for religious devotion. From Yemen, coffee continued its conquest north to the region of Hijaz, becoming popular in the cities of المدينة المنورة Al Madinah Al Munawwarah (Medina) and مكة المكرمة Makkah al-Mukarramah (Makkah/Mecca). Makkah, being the birthplace of the prophet Muhammad, the founder of Islam, was the center of the Islamic world. It was not long before the drink became popular throughout Muslim society. Coffeehouses multiplied endlessly and became community hubs for socializing and general merriment.

Coffee even became popular with the Bedouins, the Arabic nomadic people who have historically inhabited the desert. Coffee came into their society through trade, and they would cross the desert with coffee-brewing equipment and supplies strapped to their camels.

Coffee's expansion was not unfettered, however; coffee consumption and coffeehouses met with great resistance right from the start. A heated and long-running religious debate about whether coffee was حرام *haram* (forbidden by Islamic law) began in the early sixteenth century. The first ban on coffee in Makkah, in 1511, was due to the belief that coffee was intoxicating, bad for the health, and dangerous. The argument was made that coffee was an intoxicating beverage and thus forbidden by Islamic dietary law. Coffeehouses of the time did often resemble wine taverns, as Weinberg and Bealer detail in *The World of Caffeine:* "riotous brawling became a regular occurrence among caffeine-besotted coffeehouse tipplers and the people they kept awake with their late-night commotion." It probably did not help either that the Arabic word for coffee, *qahwa,* was originally used in reference to wine in old poetry.

There are many forms of Arabic poetry that date back to 600 AD. One form, the vernacular Nabaṭī poetry, is considered to be the people's poetry. Coffee, given its importance to Arabic culture, was a popular and recurring theme and, as a result, we have excellent early records of Arabic coffee. One popular story is by the great poet Mohammed bin Abdullah Al-Qadi, who describes the brewing of Arabic coffee more than 200 years ago.

In Al-Qadi's poem, the coffee beans are roasted until oil starts to appear on their surface. The beans are hand ground and transferred to a دلة *dallah* (Arabic coffee pot), which the poet describes as "shaped like a heron and painted inside so that the coffee grounds →

→ won't stain the pot." Water is added and the coffee is boiled. Once the grounds rise to the surface, it is ready to add spices. Cardamom and cloves are key, saffron if desired. The coffee can also be fragranced by the fossilized tree resin, amber. According to local sources, amber is sometimes still added to the lid of the coffee pot to give it a beautiful scent, even in recent times.

The term Arabic coffee in English generally refers to any of the traditional preparation styles of the Bedouins, those in the Arab states of the Gulf, Egypt, Palestine, Jordan, Lebanon, and more.

Initially, the Bedouins roasted their coffee beans over firewood in المحماس *al mihmas* (an iron roasting spoon with a long handle), but gradually *qahwa* came to be roasted over الكوار *al kuwar* (a clay pit with a stone plate stove). The coffee beans are hand ground in النجر *a-najr* (copper mortar and pestle), or in a hand-operated grinder. The Bedouins use a wooden mortar called المهباج *al mihbaj* (which also doubles as a Bedouin percussion instrument). Three types of *dallah* are traditionally used, which go by different names in different countries. In Saudi Arabia, the names are دلة الملقمة *Dallat Al Mulqimah* (the first pot, used to brew the coffee), دلة المهيلة *Dallat Al Muhayalah* (a second pot in which the brewed coffee is combined with the spices) and دلة المزلة *Dallat almuzla* (the pot from which the coffee is served). Palm fronds are woven together and pushed into the spout of the first *dallah* to help filter the coffee.

The term Arabic coffee in English generally refers to any of the traditional preparation styles of the Bedouins, those in the Arab states of the Gulf, Egypt, Palestine, Jordan, Lebanon, and more. The commonality is primarily in the ritual, codification, brewing equipment, and some parts of the brewing process, such as the addition of cardamom and that it is served black. Arabic coffee is also usually served with dates or other sweets.

The coffee roast level and spice additions vary widely throughout the region. In the South, ginger is frequently used. In Saudi Arabia and some other parts of the Arabian Peninsula, the beans get a very light roast, which, along with cardamom and a low coffee-to-water ratio, results in a light yellow, tea-like brew. Saffron and cloves are frequent additions here, too. In the North, the coffee is roasted until it's much darker and brewed to be stronger. In Lebanon, coffee is sometimes fragranced with orange blossom water. In Iraq and other areas of the North, coffee is cooked for long periods of time to make a concentrated syrup. This is stored in glass jars and is later used, along with more water and fresh coffee, to create a double-strength brew.

The preparation and serving customs of Arabic coffee are included in UNESCO's Intangible Cultural Heritage list. The UNESCO listing states that Arabic coffee is an important aspect of hospitality in Arab societies and is considered a ceremonial act of generosity.

There are up to 100, possibly many more, social codes associated with Arabic coffee. No meeting is possible without the serving of coffee. Normally, between one and three فناجين *fanaajin* (plural of فنجان *finjan*, a traditional Arabic small serving cup) of coffee are served, which a guest would receive and return with the right hand only. When one's cup is filled more than half, it is made clear that you are not welcome to stay for long.

The first cup (الهيف *Al-Haif,* The Test) is drunk by the host. In the past, this would prove it was not poisoned, but today, it is for the host to test the quality. The second cup (الضيف *A-Daif,* The Guest) is presented to the guest. If the guest does not drink immediately, he or she has a request to make of the host. The third cup (الكيف *Al-Kaif,* The Mood) the guest can drink or leave as he or she likes. The fourth cup (السيف *A-Saif,* The Sword) signifies military and civil alliance, and many leave this untouched because of the responsibilities that come with it. The fifth cup was known in the past as the cup of the Knight, the drinking of which is a pledge to exact revenge or go to war for the giver.

Today, Arabic coffee is of utmost cultural importance. The *dallah* is even featured on a coin in the United Arab Emirates. The *dallah* are often richly ornamented and play an important role in identity, and are often displayed in homes. The preparation and serving customs of Arabic coffee are included in UNESCO's Intangible Cultural Heritage list. The UNESCO listing states that Arabic coffee is an important aspect of hospitality in Arab societies and is considered a ceremonial act of generosity.

Though centuries-old traditions are upheld at coffee-drinking ceremonies among heads of tribes and the elderly, it is not uncommon to see less formal gatherings around a coffeepot in the Arabian Peninsula.

قهوة سعودية Saudi Qahwa

Gulf Coffee

SERVES 2–3

Coffee in Saudia Arabia and other Arab Gulf states is often roasted very lightly and scented with cardamom and sometimes saffron, cloves, or rosewater. The result is a drink light yellow to orange brown in color that is sweet and fragrant. It is often called Gulf coffee in English to differentiate it from other, darker-roasted styles of Arabic coffee.

14 g (3 tbsp) green, unroasted coffee beans (see Notes, below)

500 ml (17 fl oz) water (plus extra boiled water to warm the dallah *or serving pitcher)*

3 green cardamom pods, lightly crushed

Pinch of saffron

Dates, for serving

You will also need:
Dallah *or serving pitcher, Arabic or Turkish coffee pot, or a small saucepan*

Preheat the oven to 180°C (355°F). Spread the coffee beans on a baking sheet. Bake for 7–9 minutes, stirring often, until they are very light brown, almost still green—it is more about dehydrating them. Don't let them get darker than light peanut butter.

Remove from the oven and immediately pour onto a wooden surface. Traditionally, beans would be placed on a mat and tossed to drop the temperature quickly.

Pour some freshly boiled water into a *dallah* or serving pitcher. This will help prevent the coffee from cooling when you pour it in later.

Grind the coffee. Different households grind the beans anywhere from coarse to fine. Start somewhere in the middle and adjust to your preference over subsequent brews.

Pour the 500 ml (17 fl oz) water into an Arabic or Turkish coffee pot, or a small saucepan, and bring to a boil. Add the ground coffee, then reduce to a simmer for 10 minutes. If the coffee threatens to foam up and out of the pot or saucepan, reduce the heat a little.

Add the cardamom and simmer for 2 minutes more. Remove from heat. Empty the *dallah* or serving pitcher, and drop in a pinch of saffron. Pour the coffee through a sieve into the *dallah* or pitcher. Let the grounds settle, then pour into small cups to serve. Serve with dates.

Notes:
For this recipe, you will need to find unroasted (green) coffee. Your local coffee roaster might sell you some; otherwise, you can usually order small packets online. Arabic coffee is one of the oldest coffee brewing styles, so it's impossible to summarize the full art in one recipe. Recipes vary greatly among countries, and recipes are also passed down through families. Every household prepares coffee differently, so your own experimentation with roast level and spices is highly encouraged.

قهوة سادة Qahwa saada

SERVES 1–2

Unsweetened Arabic Coffee

Qahwa saada, literally plain coffee, is prepared unsweetened with medium- to dark-roast coffee, and flavored with cardamom. It is known as welcome coffee (because it is often served to a guest), as Northern Coffee in the South, or as Bedouin coffee because it is popular among the nomadic peoples of the desert. This style of bitter Arabic coffee is found with some regional variations across the Arabian Peninsula and Egypt, Iraq, Syria, and Jordan.

1 cup water

1 heaping tbsp medium- to dark-roast coffee
Grind size: fine

½ tsp ground cardamom

Dates, for serving

You will also need:
Arabic or Turkish-style stovetop coffee pot

Put the water in the brewing pot and bring to a boil. If you don't have a small coffee pot, just use a small saucepan. Add the coffee, then reduce to a simmer for 10 minutes.

If the coffee threatens to foam up and out of the pot, lift the pot off the heat until the foam subsides then return it to the heat. You may need to do this multiple times.

Add the cardamom and simmer for 2 minutes more. Remove from the heat.

Let the grounds settle for a few moments. To serve, pour into small cups. Serve with dates.

Notes:
Different households, regions, and countries prepare this coffee very differently. Orange flower water or rosewater can be added, or it can be flavored with cinnamon, cloves, and ginger. Some brew it with sugar or serve it with sugar on the side. In Iraq, the coffee is sometimes boiled for a much longer time, creating a strong, concentrated coffee essence.

Community in Turkey's Coffeehouses

Circa 1550, Istanbul: Ottoman coffeehouses began opening, quickly becoming popular community gathering places—and causing a decrease in attendance at mosques.

The Ottoman Empire controlled or had an administrative presence in much of southeastern Europe, North Africa, and western Asia for much of the second millennium. Founded in the 1300s, the capital of the Empire was, for the majority of the era, Istanbul. Historians believe that *kahve* (coffee) was introduced to Turkish society after the Ottoman Empire seized Yemen in 1538, during the reign of Sultan Süleyman (known as Suleiman the Magnificent in the West). In Yemen, members of mystical orders, or Sufis, drank coffee to stay awake for their nightly religious devotions. Others believe it may have arrived in Turkey via Egypt (ruled by the Ottomans since 1517) where coffee is believed to have been introduced a few decades earlier.

Cemal Kafadar, professor of Turkish studies at Harvard University, notes in his essay *How Dark is the History of the Night, How Black the Story of Coffee, How Bitter the Tale of Love: The Changing Measure of Leisure and Pleasure in Early Modern Istanbul* that the earliest mention found, thus far, of coffee in Istanbul was in 1539. A grand admiral registered property that included a *kahve odası*, a Turkish coffee room or chamber. Kafadar also notes that the Ottoman historian İbrahim Peçevi's records around a century later are widely accepted to detail the first *kahvehanes* (coffeehouses) in Istanbul, which Peçevi said started to appear around the 1550s.

Ottoman coffeehouses quickly became part of the everyday fabric of society. They were secular spaces, providing a "third place" for men from various ethnic and religious backgrounds to meet, discuss, and share stories and knowledge. Coffee's stimulating effects were beloved in Ottoman society—and the caffeinated fervor of these places was a key draw. Packed with intellectuals, writers, businessmen, dissidents, and spies, coffeehouses were meeting places, hothouses of debate, and community gathering spaces.

The Turkish brewing method results in an extremely hot, strong coffee filled with *telve* (coffee sediment), which needs to settle before the drink is sipped. It was drunk without milk, and initially without sugar, which was not widely available at the time. Drinking coffee was not supposed to be done on the go—the development of the coffeehouse created a dedicated space in which to sit and enjoy your brew with leisure.

Gradually, as the *kahvehanes* became a central part of Ottoman social life, some religious men became displeased at the decreased attendance at mosques. Peçevi states in his seventeenth-century record of the Ottoman Empire, *Tarih-i Peçevi* (*Pecevi's History*), that "the Imams and muezzins and pious hypocrites said: 'people have become addicts of the coffeehouse; nobody comes to the mosques!' The *ulema* (Muslim scholars with specialist knowledge of Islamic law) said, 'It is a house of evil deeds; it is better to go to the wine tavern than there.' The preachers, in particular, made great efforts to forbid it."

Throughout the seventeenth century, the government linked periods of social unrest to coffeehouses. They believed that seeds of discontent were →

CERAMIC ART GALLERY
ŞARK HALICILIK
STORE
CERAMIC ART GALLERY
HAREM 47
Tel:518 36 07
VESTEL
VESTEL

BARIS CAFE
LIMITS OFF

→ sown in these public spaces, which they viewed as nonhierarchical and allowing interaction between diverse groups. The news was read out loud, informing and educating the illiterate. Gossip about the palace spread. Acts of revolt against the Sultan were planned. Government agents believed that this uncontrollable interaction presented a threat to the social order. Thus, for religious and social reasons, coffeehouses were banned from time to time in an attempt to limit their proliferation and influence. These bans were largely ignored, reversed, and reenacted several times, and the consumption of coffee continued to increase.

Turkish coffee is brewed by bringing very finely-ground coffee and water just to a boil in a *cezve.* It is usually brewed on a stovetop now, but traditionally it was heated over coals.

During the rule of sultans who were not opposed to the brew, coffee grew to be popular in the palace. Hakan Karateke, Professor of Ottoman and Turkish Culture, Language, and Literature at the University of Chicago, says that the palace would have a number of dedicated coffee masters. The *kahvecibaşı* (the chief coffee maker) would, with his attendants, serve coffee to the "men of the state." He was also responsible for the upkeep of the precious items used in preparing coffee: ornate brewing pots, cups, trays, embroidered cloths. The *kahveci usta* (mistress of the coffee service) attended to the coffee only in the Sultan's private apartments.

In the Ottoman era, coffee was usually drunk black, unsweetened. Today, flavorings popular in Iran, Greece, and the Arabian Peninsula, such as mastic, cinnamon, anise, and cloves, are used in Turkey, too. Nowadays, Turkish coffee is often drunk sweet: when you order, you must specify *çok şekerli* (sweet), *orta şekerli* (medium sweet), *az şekerli* (minimal sugar) or *sade* (plain). Another relatively modern accompaniment is the rose-scented *lokum* (Turkish delight), a chewy sweet companion served alongside the intense brew. Karateke remembers cherry and lemon liquor being served with coffee on festival days in his youth, although not so often anymore.

Turkish coffee is brewed by bringing very finely-ground coffee and water just to a boil in a *cezve* (a specialized long-handled brewing pot traditionally made from brass or copper). It is usually brewed on a stovetop now, but traditionally it was heated over coals.

The quality of the equipment determines the taste of the coffee. The hourglass shape of the *cezve* is important: it allows the coffee to be poured easily, creating a sort of funnel as it is tipped, directing a thin stream out of the spout into the *fincan* (small cups, often made from glass or porcelain, or from metal such as copper). The *fincan* were often placed into an ornate metal holder called a *zarf,* which provides a handle to hold the hot cup.

The shape of the *cezve* neck filters out some of the coffee grounds as the liquid is poured. More importantly, the narrowed neck is crucial for developing foam, necessary for the proper brewing of Turkish coffee. The temperature and foaming of the coffee are managed by lifting the pot on and off the heat source.

Tadeusz Krusiński, a Polish Jesuit who lived in and chronicled late Safavid Iran during the 1700s, published a key text detailing coffee drinking in the Ottoman Empire. *Pragmatographia de legitimo usu Ambrozyi Tureckiey* (*Description of the Proper Manner of Taking Turkish Coffee*), as translated by Anna Malecka, notes that coffee was boiled until thick (*ağır kahve*, heavy coffee), but that "the more refined…do not drink coffee until it settles." Krusiński then details a →

→ long-forgotten method of using a sprinkling of grated deer horn to help the grinds settle faster.

The coffee grinds left at the bottom of the cup have a secondary use in Turkish culture. According to Yeşim Gökçe in an article published by the Turkish Cultural Foundation, *kahve falı* (coffee fortune-telling), has been practiced for centuries. A saucer is placed over a finished cup of coffee, inverted, and left to cool. Someone other than the drinker, a friend or a professional, will then interpret the shapes left behind by the coffee grounds, reading the past and divining the future of the drinker.

This dark, intense coffee should not be drunk on an empty stomach, according to Turkish custom. For this reason, the Turkish word for breakfast is *kahvaltı*—*kahve* meaning coffee, *altı* meaning under, in this context generally accepted as *before coffee.* This isn't the only way the Turkish love of coffee has pervaded language: the color brown in Turkish is *kahverengi*, which translates literally to the color of coffee.

Locals enjoy Turkish coffee on Pierre Loti hill, Istanbul. Offering a spectacular panoramic view of Istanbul's seven hills, the cafe draws tourists seeking coffee in the traditional style.

Türk Kahvesi

Turkish Coffee

Turkish coffee is served black, often with a generous helping of sugar. A long-handled brewing pot called a *cezve* is required to brew it properly, which can be easily found online (often called a Turkish coffee pot). Turkish coffee is commonly served in a small cup alongside a glass of water and a piece of *lokum* (Turkish delight).

90 ml (3 fl oz) water

7 g (1 heaping tbsp) light- to medium-roast coffee
Grind size: Turkish fine (extremely fine, like powdered sugar)

1 tsp granulated sugar, or to taste

Turkish delights, for serving

You will also need:
Cezve (Turkish coffee brewing pot), specialty Turkish coffee grinder or a manual burr coffee grinder (see Notes, below)

Pour the water into the *cezve*, and heat on the stove on a high heat to approximately 60°C (140°F); test using a thermometer.

Sprinkle the coffee onto the surface of the hot water; do not stir in. Add the sugar. When the coffee starts to sink, stir, turn down the heat to low.

The liquid will begin to foam, so manage it carefully. Remove the *cezve* from the heat for a moment, or turn the heat down even lower to keep the bubbles very small.

Do not let the liquid boil. Instead, let a thick froth build. When the froth starts to rise up the neck of the pot, remove the *cezve* from the heat once the foam almost reaches the top.

If you've brewed more than one serving, pour a little into each cup to distribute the foam and then repeat to fill the cups.

Wait for the foam and coffee sediment to settle before drinking.

Serve with some Turkish delight.

Notes:
If you are using pre-ground coffee powder, you will need to repeat the heating and cooling step to build lasting froth. After you remove the *cezve* from the heat, the froth will subside: return it to the heat, then repeat the rise and cool process once or twice more. If your coffee is fresh, only one rise should be required to build a lasting froth. Blade and burr domestic grinders are rarely able to grind coffee finely enough for Turkish coffee. If you can't find a Turkish grinder, try to find a manual burr grinder (which works in a similar way to a pepper mill) and grind as finely as you can manage.

Smuggled Beans and Monsoon Winds in India

1600s, Karnataka: a popular coffee legend says that Sufi saint Baba Budan smuggled coffee back from his pilgrimage to Makkah, thus breaking the Arabic stronghold on coffee production.

The story of India's coffee history often opens with a captivating legend: Sufi saint Baba Budan broke the Yemeni monopoly on coffee production by smuggling seven coffee seeds (a symbolic number in Islam) out of Yemen to his home in Chikmagalur, Karnataka. Some legends say they were hidden in his beard; others say they were strapped to his chest.

While the exact moment coffee first reached India's shores is unclear, it is highly likely that Indian traders and merchants first encountered coffee as it began to proliferate throughout the Arabian Peninsula and the Islamic World. Trade between India and the Arabian Peninsula has existed since ancient times.

Some sources hypothesize that if not Baba Budan, it may have been early Arab traders who first brought coffee plants to India, while others begin the telling of India's coffee-cultivation story with seventeenth-century Dutch experiments in Malabar. Many focus on the colonial connection; the Coffee Board of India, which promotes coffee production in India, records that large commercial plantations began in the 1800s after "British colonial entrepreneurs conquered the hostile forest terrain in South India." However, researcher Bhaswati Bhattacharya states in her paper *Local History of a Global Commodity: Production of Coffee in Mysore and Coorg in the Nineteenth Century* that local growers in key areas far outnumbered European growers, at least until the end of the nineteenth century.

So it wasn't only the colonial powers who were interested in coffee. While India is often considered a tea-drinking nation, coffee was also a popular drink all the way back in seventeenth-century Mughal India. Historian Stephen P. Blake notes in his book *Shahjahanabad, The Sovereign City in Mughal India 1639–1739* that Old Delhi was filled with *qahwakhanas* (from the Arabic قهوة *qahwa*, coffee).

At times, India's coffee industry was supported by an enterprising government. Bhattacharya notes in her book *Much Ado Over Coffee: Indian Coffee House Then and Now* that in between the Great Depression and the Second World War, colonial economic policy resulted in an export surplus. To support the coffee industry, the government set up an organization called the Indian Coffee Cess Committee, with the goal of marketing Indian coffee at home and abroad. To help sell the surplus coffee, they opened up a chain of cafés called the Indian Coffee House across the country; the first was in Bombay in 1936. In the 1950s, these were scheduled to be closed down—until the workers convinced the Coffee Board to hand over ownership. To this day, the workers run the Indian Coffee Houses through a number of cooperatives throughout the country.

These establishments have been referred to as India's Living Room. Sankurshan Thakur writes in his book *The Brothers Bihari*, "the Indian Coffee House was where I heard words like *führer* and fascism first, words like *proletariat* and *bourgeoisie*."

These days, over 70 percent of India's coffee crop is bound for export. While it would seem this would leave little for domestic consumption in a country →

CHAITHRAM
GOVT. OF KERALA UNDERTAKING
INDIAN COFFEE HOUSE
INDIA COFFEE BOARD WORKERS CO-OPERATIVE SOCIETY LTD. NO. 4227
A/C BAR
INDIAN COFFEE HOUSE
INDIAN COFFEE HOUSE
NO PARKING
kvb e-flash
INSTANT MONEY
A.K.T.A
2010
CITY
K.S.R.T.C. Stall No.
KILLIPALAM CHICKEN CORNER
JUICE
Robsta
USA

NI RESTAURANT & BAKERY
RESTAURANT
& BAKERY
यजदानी रेस्टॉरन्ट अँड बेकरी
La BouLangerie
YAZDANI BAKERY
SINCE 1950
FRESH
APPLE PIE
BREADS

→ so large, India has a strong and vibrant coffee culture—particularly in the South, which is where three-quarters of the country's coffee is consumed annually.

So how is coffee usually consumed in India today? The traditional way of brewing in the South is called *meter kaapi*, *Kumbakonam* degree coffee, *Mysore* filter, or *Mylapore* filter, depending on whom you ask.

In southern India, spices are often blended in with the coffee. India is the second-largest cardamom producer in the world, so it is not uncommon to find a few pods added to your French press.

Kaapi—loanword, from coffee—is brewed in a special filter that consists of two cups, one that nests on top of the other. The upper cup holds the coffee grounds and a pressing disc for tamping, and it has many small holes that allow the brew to drip down. The strong brew is mixed with milk and sugar, and poured into a *dabara*—a traditional Madras-style tumbler.

When it comes to the bean itself, India's sheer size and variety of climates provide fertile ground for coffee growing. There is a range of varieties and styles grown across the country.

Pouring the coffee back and forth between the tumbler and the serving saucer blends, emulsifies, and cools it, aerating it without adding the extra water that a steam wand would add. The flavor is indeed different than if you had simply stirred it all together. This pouring back and forth is how South Indian filter coffee earned the name *meter kaapi* because the drink is often poured into the saucer from a meter height.

The coffee is often blended with chicory root, roasted, then ground. The chicory holds onto the hot water for a little longer while it is brewing, resulting in a stronger extraction with a thicker mouthfeel.

In southern India, spices are often blended in with the coffee. India is the second-largest cardamom producer in the world, so it is not uncommon to find a few pods added to your French press.

Although fresh brewed coffee is best loved, many in India also adore the nostalgic cold coffee, which is made by whizzing up instant coffee or a 3-in-1 packet in a blender with milk, ice, extra sugar, and sometimes ice cream.

When it comes to the bean itself, India's sheer size and variety of climates provide fertile ground for coffee growing. There is a range of varieties and styles grown across the country, and one unique processing style now has protected status under India's Geographical Indications of Goods Act. The revered Monsooned Malabar is made by exposing the raw coffee to monsoon winds, which changes the color and imparts a characteristic flavor and a mellowed acidity.

The Indian Coffee House currently runs as many as 400 establishments in India, including the distinctive brickwork spiral in Trivandrum, Kerala (page 89) and a large drinking hall in Kolkata, West Bengal (page 93, top).

NO ADMISSION
The reason for my charming smile
INDIAN COFFEE

KINDLY REQUEST YOU TO GIVE THE
YOUR LAUGAGE YOUR

Filter Kaapi

SERVES 2

Filter Coffee

In other parts of India, *chai* (tea) is king, but in southern India, filter *kaapi* rules. It's called *meter kaapi* because the coffee maker blends and froths the drink by pouring it between cups from a meter high. Chicory isn't always used but high-quality coffee is. Try it with a peaberry (see page 265) blend.

25 g (5 level tbsp) coffee blend:
80 percent medium-roast coffee,
20 percent ground roasted chicory
Grind size: fine

180 g (6 ½ oz) hot water
(93°C–96°C/200°F–205°F)

1 cup milk

Sugar to taste

You will also need:
Indian-style coffee filter (see Notes, below), dabara *tumbler and saucer, or two metal cups*

Put the ground-coffee blend into the top chamber of the Indian-style coffee filter, distribute evenly, and using the perforated insert, tamp down lightly, then leave the filter in place. Place the whole apparatus over a scale, and press tare to reset to zero.

Add 40 g (1 ½ oz) water—just enough to wet the grounds. Replace the lid on the filter, leave for 15 seconds, then proceed to fill the top chamber with the hot water until the scales read 180 g (6 ½ oz). Cover and leave for up to 20 minutes to allow for the coffee to filter through—this brewed coffee is known as the "decoction."

Meanwhile, heat the milk in a saucepan. As it begins to foam, remove from the heat and pour from the highest distance you can into another vessel large enough to hold the liquid without splashing too much. This will froth the milk and prevent a skin from forming on top.

Pour some coffee decoction into the *dabara* tumbler, then top up with as much milk as you'd like. Add sugar to taste.

Pour the mixture between the *dabara* tumbler and its saucer, from as high of a distance as you can manage (this aerates the milk, mixes the sugar, and emulsifies it). Repeat a few times until it's blended, creamy, and frothy.

Notes:
No Indian coffee filter? Combine coffee and water in a metal pitcher, cover for 30 seconds, stir, and cover again. Leave for 1–2 minutes, then strain through a cheesecloth or fine sieve. Chicory is a tough root that you won't want to put in your coffee grinder. If making your own chicory-coffee blend, buy roasted chicory, already finely ground. If the coffee filter isn't brand new, sit the top half over a low flame to burn off old coffee residue. Handle carefully because the metal will become very hot.

Chukku Kaapi

SERVES
2–3

Ginger Coffee

In Kerala, you'll find *chukku kaapi*, in Tamil Nadu, *karupatti kaapi*. Both are sweetened with jaggery and often spiced. *Chukku* means ginger in Malayalam (the language spoken in Kerala by the Malayali people), *karupatti* means jaggery in Tamil. This spicy-sweet brew clears the sinuses and is often used as an Ayurvedic remedy for coughs or colds.

700 ml (24 fl oz) water

3 tbsp jaggery or brown sugar

1½ tsp ginger powder

¼ tsp ground black pepper

2 green cardamom pods, slightly crushed

½ tsp cumin seeds

1 tbsp dried tulsi *(holy basil) or*
10 leaves of fresh tulsi

1 heaping tbsp medium-roast coffee
Grind size: medium

Bring the water to a boil in a saucepan. Add the jaggery or brown sugar (you don't need to use all of it if you'd like it less sweet) and stir until dissolved.

Add the ginger, black pepper, cardamom, and cumin. Leave to simmer covered for 5 minutes. Turn down the heat to low, add the *tulsi* and the coffee, stir, and then cover again, leaving to simmer for a further 2–3 minutes.

Strain through a cheesecloth or sieve into serving cups, and serve hot.

Notes:

While both *chukku* and *karupatti kaapi* are sweetened with jaggery, sometimes *karupatti kaapi* is just made with jaggery, no spices. *Chukku kaapi* is also sometimes only brewed with jaggery and ginger, but in other recipes, other spices are added—the recipe varies by region and from household to household. Some people add coriander seed or clove, so feel free to experiment.

Cold Coffee

This easy iced coffee recipe is a necessity for the hot Indian summer. It's essentially just a coffee milkshake and can be found in cafés all over India. Given how easy it is to prepare, it's frequently made at home, and many remember it as the ultimate nostalgic Desi drink of their childhoods.

1 tbsp instant coffee

2 tbsp hot water

½ tbsp sugar (or to taste)

1½ cups whole milk

¼ cup vanilla ice cream

Put the instant coffee into a blender, then pour the hot water over it to dissolve.

Add the sugar, and pulse the blender a few times until the sugar and coffee mixture is a little frothy and the sugar is blended in.

Add the milk and ice cream, and blend for 1–2 minutes until very frothy.

Notes:

For the quintessential cold coffee flavor and consistency, instant coffee and sugar are important. The dehydration process the instant coffee goes through results in a creamier, foamier beverage once blended. Sugar increases the viscosity, holding the foaminess for longer. You can of course use espresso or strong coffee to make this if you would prefer not to use instant, but the consistency will be different. Some omit the ice cream or use 3-in-1 packets that are readily found in grocery stores across Asia, instead of the coffee, sugar, and ice cream. Cold coffee made with the 3-in-1 mixture should be blended longer, for 2–3 minutes because the longer you blend it, the creamier it gets.

Cultivation and Creativity in Java's Spiritual Home

1696, Dutch East Indies: *Arabica* coffee was planted on the island of Java, initiating centuries of coffee culture and cultivation across modern-day Indonesia's roughly 12,000 inhabited islands.

It is no coincidence that a colloquial name for coffee—java—is also the name of one of Indonesia's largest islands. Indonesia has long played a starring role in coffee's history. The largest archipelago in the world, Indonesia comprises 17,508 islands, of which about 12,000 are inhabited. The country is home to more than 300 ethnicities and cultures, and there are hundreds of traditional coffee-growing, harvesting, processing, and brewing methods, many of which have been passed down through generations.

Historians believe the Dutch introduced coffee to the island of Java in the 1690s. Some plants cultivated on the island were sent to Hortus Botanicus botanical gardens in Amsterdam, and from there were gifted to the King of France. A seedling sent to the French colony of Martinique proliferated, becoming the progenitor of a reported 18 million coffee trees over the course of the next 50 years. The majority of coffee trees grown across the Caribbean, South America, and Central America have their roots in Java.

Coffee cultivation was a success in Java too, leading to the development of coffee plantations across other islands including Sumatra, Sulawesi, and Bali. Initially, all cultivated coffee was of the *arabica* species, which is revered for its depth of flavor and its quality. But in the mid-1800s, a fungal disease called coffee rust was discovered in East Africa. By 1876, the devastating disease had spread to coffee plantations across Indonesia.

The Dutch introduced two other species, *liberica* and *canephora (robusta)*, the latter of which fared much better than *arabica* against the disease, and proved easier to grow. As a result, today the majority of Indonesia's coffee production is *robusta*, and the country is one of the world's leading *robusta* producers. *Liberica* is still grown to satisfy local demand.

The island of Sumatra is famous for its *arabica* coffees, which have a unique flavor, often heavy-bodied and earthy, with low acidity. The taste is largely the result of a traditional processing technique called *giling basah*, a wet hulling process native to the region.

Indonesia has become famed for *kopi luwak*, or civet coffee. The fresh, ripe coffee cherries are first eaten, digested, and then defecated by a small mammal called a palm civet, after which the beans are collected and processed. Not quite as well known is *kopi toratima*, produced on the island of Sulawesi. Nocturnal marsupials select ripe coffee cherries, eat the fruit, then spit out the beans for the farmers to collect from the forest floor.

Indonesia plays a prominent and invaluable role in coffee history, yet the dark side of colonial exploitation cannot be ignored. The coffee trade was highly profitable for the Dutch, but coffee production certainly did not always improve local farmers' lives.

Around 1830, the Dutch governor-general mandated the government policy of *Cultuurstelsel*, referred to by Indonesian historians as *Tanam Paksa* (Enforced Planting). The revenue-raising policy was intended to exploit the Dutch East Indies' resources and dig the Dutch out of a dire financial situation brought about →

→ by a series of wars. The people of Java were forced to set aside a portion of their arable land to plant specific commercial crops, such as coffee, for the colonial government. Prior to the implementation of the *Cultuurstelsel,* the Dutch had already been enforcing coffee planting in Parahyangan (Preanger), West Java (the homeland of the Sundanese people) since the early 1700s, through the *Preangerstelsel.*

Indonesia plays a prominent and invaluable role in coffee history, yet the dark side of colonial exploitation cannot be ignored. The coffee trade was highly profitable for the Dutch, but coffee production certainly did not always improve local farmers' lives.

Across the Dutch East Indies, subsistence farmers found themselves with fields filled with crops bound for export. Villagers were legally tethered to their land and often reduced to destitution: when crops failed or disease struck, many suffered from successive famines.

When news of their predicament spread to the Netherlands, people cried out for reform. *Cultuurstelsel* was gradually dismantled during the mid- to late-1800s, and in 1870, the Agrarian Law, passed by the Dutch, decreed that only Indonesians could own land although foreigners could lease it from them. But it wasn't until the 1945 Proclamation of Indonesian Independence that some local farmers began to take ownership of private plantation areas.

For generations, Indonesians have incorporated coffee into their daily lives, leading to an incredibly diverse coffee culture. Open-pan roasting was common (and still is in some small villages and rural areas). Coffee is roasted in a wok over a wood fire, then crushed by hand in a large wood mill. Regional variations add a slice of old coconut to the pan, while others add corn kernels, rice, sticky rice, or mung beans.

During the colonial era, many roaster businesses were owned by upper-middle-class people of Chinese descent. These *koffie fabrieks* (Dutch for coffee factories) sold *kopi bubuk* (coffee powder). They imported roasting machines from Europe, many of which are still used by the fourth- or fifth-generation owners of these businesses today.

These days, coffee is usually bought from street vendors or at small neighborhood coffee shops. They may go by different names (*keude kupi* in Aceh, *warung kopi* in Java and Bali, or sometimes *kedai kopi* in Sumatra), but these shops all share a similar culture of sipping coffee, sharing conversation, and watching the world go by.

In Yogyakarta, in the South of Java, a piece of hot charcoal is added to black coffee to create *kopi joss,* the theory being that the charcoal reduces the acidity of the coffee and makes it easier on the stomach.

Indonesian coffee is made in a variety of styles. Basic brewed coffee is called *kopi tubruk,* made by simply pouring hot water over coffee grounds. In the oil- and teak-producing regions of Central Java, *kopi kuthuk* is coffee that has been boiled with sugar until it's very thick. In the city of Tulungagung in East Java, *kopi ijo* (green coffee) is popular. Coffee shop owners receive their coffee in unroasted form and roast it lightly in a clay wok. The resulting drink has a green hue when brewed.

Kopi telur (or *kopi talua*), or egg coffee, is drunk throughout West Sumatra. Hot, sweet coffee is poured →

→ over a whipped egg yolk, topped with a slice of lime, and sometimes a dash of vanilla. Also in West Sumatra, the Minangkabau people make *kawa daun.* They dry and roast coffee leaves, steeping them to make a coffee leaf tea. In Yogyakarta, in the South of Java, a piece of hot charcoal is added to black coffee to create *kopi joss,* the theory being that the charcoal reduces the acidity of the coffee and makes it easier on the stomach.

In Lasem, a northern coastal town in Central Java, men drink their *kopi tubruk,* pat down the grounds to remove excess moisture, then mix the grounds with condensed milk to make a paste. Using a toothpick or a spoon, they use the paste to decorate cigarettes with beautifully delicate patterns, such as stylized flowers and batik motifs. This type of folk art is called *ngelelet* in Lasem or *nyethe* in other parts of Java. When the decoration is dry, the cigarette can be smoked. The coffee is said to give a spicy flavor to the tobacco.

At the coffee plantation in Western Java featured on these pages, all stages of coffee growing, harvesting, and drying are done by hand—right down to selecting the beans for roasting.

Kopi Rarobang

SERVES 2

Ginger and Nut Coffee

Ginger coffee is drunk in many regions of Indonesia, going by the name *kopi halia, kopi jahe,* or *kopi goraka.* The Maluku Islands (the Moluccas) are often referred to as Indonesia's "spice islands," as popular culinary spices, like nutmeg and clove, are native to there. *Kopi rarobang* is a coffee typical of the capital, Ambon City. The sweet, hot drink has an added crunch, as it is topped with sliced *kenari* nuts, a locally grown wild nut.

2 cups water

30 g (1 oz) fresh ginger, sliced

1 small cinnamon stick

2 cloves

1 pandan leaf

40 g (3 tbsp) granulated sugar

2 heaping tbsp coffee
Grind size: medium

1 tbsp shelled kenari (pili) *nuts*
(see Notes, below)

Put the water, ginger, cinnamon, cloves, and pandan leaf in a pan set over a medium-high heat, stir, cover, and bring to a boil. Continue boiling until it takes on a light golden color, about 10 minutes.

Add the sugar to the pan and stir to dissolve. Bring the liquid back to a boil, then reduce heat and add the ground coffee. Stir until it comes to a gentle simmer, then remove the pan from the heat.

Leave to infuse while you heat a separate small pan. Slice the *kenari* or *pili* nuts and toast in the pan until golden. Pour the coffee through a small sieve into serving cups, then top with the toasted nuts.

Notes:

Traditionally, *kopi rarobang* is made using the *kenari* nut, native to eastern Indonesia. Often referred to as an Indonesian walnut, it is very different from a common walnut. The *pili* nut is a great substitute. More easily found outside of Indonesia, the *pili* nut is from a species of tree in the same genus—in fact, *pili* nuts are also called *kenari* in Indonesia. Otherwise, pine nuts are the next best option.

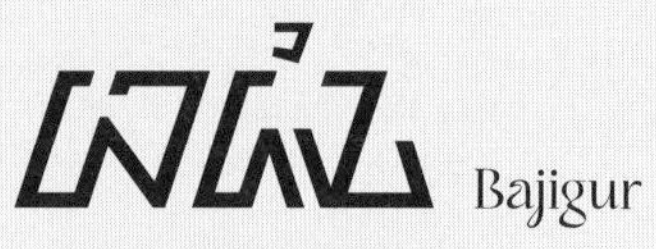

Bajigur

Spiced Coconut Milk

SERVES 2–3

Bajigur is a coconut milk-based drink, native to the Sundanese people of West Java. It was traditionally sold by hawkers carrying a long bamboo pole with a container hanging from each side—one filled with hot *bajigur*, the other with boiled fruits, beans, and nuts to be eaten alongside.

30 g (1 oz) fresh ginger

1 cup coconut milk

1 cup water

40 g (3 ½ tbsp) palm sugar, thinly sliced if solid, or brown sugar

1 pandan leaf, knotted

1 small cinnamon stick

1 heaping tsp coffee
Grind size: medium

Pinch of salt

Using metal tongs, grill the ginger directly over a gas flame until small areas of char show (if you don't have a gas flame, you can skip this step.) Using a mallet or a pestle, crush the ginger until it releases some of its juice.

Pour the coconut milk and water into a small pan, then add the ginger, palm sugar, pandan, cinnamon, ground coffee, and salt.

Over low heat, continually stir, slowly, to ensure the coconut milk does not split. When small bubbles form on the surface, remove the pan from the heat and transfer the ginger, cinnamon, and pandan to a heatproof glass jug. Carefully strain the *bajigur* into the jug.

Notes:

Bajigur doesn't traditionally contain coffee, but like many recipes, it has been subjected to variations and differences across households and regions. These days, coffee is a common inclusion. Some recipes also call for the addition of young coconut or toddy palm fruit, while others add lemongrass or omit the cinnamon.

Es Kopi Apulkat

SERVES 1

Iced Avocado Coffee

Although usually used in Europe and North America as a vegetable, avocado is really a fruit. In Asia and Central and South America, it is often used in smoothies and sweet dishes. In Indonesia, it is blended with coffee and condensed milk and served over ice or blended with ice, for a cool, refreshing smoothie.

1 extra-large ripe avocado

4 tbsp sweetened condensed milk

80–100 g ice (3 large ice cubes)

¼–½ cup fresh cow's milk, or coconut milk

A drizzle of chocolate-flavored sweetened condensed milk (see Notes, below)

60 ml (2 fl oz) espresso, cooled, or 4 heaping tsp instant coffee mixed with ¼ cup water

1–2 scoops ice cream

You will also need:
Blender

Scoop out the avocado flesh and put it in a blender, along with the sweetened condensed milk, ice, and ¼ cup of milk or coconut milk.

Blend until it reaches smoothie consistency; you should be able to pour it easily. Add more milk if it's too thick (this will depend on the size of your avocado).

Drizzle some chocolate-flavored condensed milk (or chocolate syrup) around the inside of a serving glass just before pouring the avocado smoothie in. Top with espresso or instant coffee mixed with water.

Place a scoop of ice cream on top, and if you like, drizzle with more chocolate condensed milk.

Notes:
In some places, you'll find everything whizzed together in a blender, but modern coffee shops in Indonesia are now serving this traditional drink *affogato* style, like the recipe above. If you can't find chocolate-flavored condensed milk, you can substitute chocolate syrup.

Kopi Serai

SERVES 1

Lemongrass Coffee

Kopi serai, lemongrass coffee, is drunk throughout Indonesia. It is sometimes flavored with other spices or called by different names. This basic recipe for lemongrass coffee is made with ginger, too, to create a lovely, well-balanced flavor. In Indonesia, the local red ginger is often used, which has a stronger, peppery bite compared to white ginger.

1 cup water

1 stalk lemongrass, bruised and chopped

Small piece fresh root ginger (preferably red)

1½ tbsp granulated sugar

2 level tbsp coffee
Grind size: medium

Put the water, lemongrass, ginger, and sugar in a saucepan (use one with a lid) over a high heat. Bring to a boil, stirring until the sugar is melted. Cover the pan with the lid, turn the heat to low, and continue to simmer for 10 minutes. Remove the pan from the heat.

Add the ground coffee to the pan. Leave to infuse for 3–4 minutes, then pour through a cloth filter or a fine-mesh sieve into a cup to serve.

Notes:

Across Indonesia's roughly 12,000 inhabited islands, spices and fruits are often added to coffee, so there are many different names for similar drinks. In East Java, a lemongrass coffee is made by adding coffee to the traditional *wedang pokak* drink, an infusion of red ginger, cloves, cinnamon, pandan, lemongrass, and other spices. *Kopi rempah* (spiced coffee) is usually made from the same ingredients, although either Javanese chili, black pepper, or *kapulaga* (white, round Javanese cardamom) is added too. Try your own mix of spices and sugar to find a version you like.

Coffee's Stepping Stone to the New World

1492, Kingdom of Castile: Christopher Columbus set sail from Spain and made landfall in the Americas, thus beginning a long period of transatlantic colonization and transfer of people and crops.

It is unclear when coffee was first introduced to Spain. Perhaps it was during the al-Andalus period, when much of Spain and Portugal were under Muslim rule for more than 700 years from 711 AD. Towards the end of this period, coffee was beginning to quickly spread throughout the Arabian Peninsula and Muslim society, so it is feasible that coffee also touched Spain's shores. Other stories tell of Turkish immigrants popularizing coffee, while later we see records of coffee being drunk in the "French fashion" all across Spain and Portugal. We do know that coffee's spread across Europe and its colonies was unstoppable during the mid-late second millennium. Yet, coffee didn't make as many waves in Spain as it did in much of the rest of Europe, at least initially—the Spanish much preferred to drink chocolate and wine.

However, Spanish ships carried coffee plants to many corners of the world. During the Spanish colonization of the Americas, from the late fifteenth century through to the early nineteenth century, the Spanish empire expanded into most of Central America, much of North and South America, and many islands of the Caribbean. In 1492, a voyage west led by Christopher Columbus made the first connection between Europe and the Americas. Columbus was funded by the Kingdom of Castile (now a part of Spain) and paved the way for Spanish conquistadors to establish trade routes, and open the Americas to Spanish and other European colonization.

The exchange of plants, crops, ideas, technology (and disease) between the continents over the subsequent centuries became known as the Columbian Exchange. Coffee was largely introduced across the Americas and the Caribbean by European explorers and colonizers, including the Spanish. In the eighteenth century, Spanish colonists planted the first coffee in Mexico, while in Guatemala, another leading modern coffee-growing country, the first plants were likely introduced by Spanish Jesuits. Spanish missionaries took coffee plants from Mexico and introduced them to the Philippines in the late 1700s, too. Back in Spain, coffee consumption grew, albeit slowly. Spain and Portugal had extended their colonial reach into Africa, which was much more convenient for colonial coffee cultivation.

While we aren't certain who was the first to add milk to coffee, the Spanish had been adding milk to hot chocolate since the early sixteenth century. It is, therefore, no surprise that the *café con leche* (coffee with milk) became one of Spain's most-popular coffee drinks and spread quickly to other Spanish-speaking countries, where it is still popular today.

The *café con leche* is usually a 1:1 mix of hot milk and black coffee—no foam. The ratio of milk and coffee can be adjusted: asking for a *café manchado* adds more milk, while the *café cortado* has less milk. The *café solo* is a black coffee, like espresso, and the *café bombon* is a *café solo* with sweetened condensed milk, invented in Valencia. At home, most Spanish households brew with a *cafetera*, an Italian-style stovetop →

VEN A
nuestro
CUPPING
SEMANAL
ORIGINS
TIME
3:30
Solo
TANTUM
Largo
LONGUM
Semi Largo
SEMILONGUM
Solo Corto
TANTUMTANTILLUM
Mitad
NE QUID NIMIS
Entre Corto
IN MEDIAS RES
Corto
TANTILLUM
Sombra
UMBRACULUM
Nube
NUBECULA
No me lo ponga
HORROR VACUI

→ brewer (see page 39). It's also common for alcohol to be added to coffee. The *carajillo* is drunk across the country, and has numerous regional variations; the basic *carajillo* is coffee, brandy, lemon peel, and sugar.

Spanish ships carried coffee plants to many corners of the world. During the Spanish colonization of the Americas, the Spanish empire expanded into most of Central America, much of North and South America, and many islands of the Caribbean.

Many travelers to Spain notice a difference in flavor between a *café solo* and an espresso elsewhere, despite the similarities visually. Few know that this is because of a process that happens before the coffee even reaches the coffee shop. The *torrefacto* (which simply means roasted in Spanish) method is said to have become popular during the Spanish Civil War when imports of coffee became scarce.

While we aren't certain who was the first to add milk to coffee, the Spanish had been adding milk to hot chocolate since the early sixteenth century. It is, therefore, no surprise that the *café con leche* (coffee with milk) became one of Spain's most-popular coffee drinks.

In the *torrefacto* method, coffee beans are coated in a layer of burnt sugar, which increases the volume of the coffee by up to 20 percent. Roasters in a number of countries around the world employ this sugar-coating method, claiming that it prevents the beans from oxidizing, compensates for evaporation, and masks the flavor of inferior quality beans.

Torrefacto roasted beans produce a very dark coffee, a thick *crema,* and a bitter taste. Much like in Southeast Asia, this style of roasting has pervaded Spanish coffee culture and influenced taste; the *torrefacto* roast remains popular to this day. Even with the rise of specialty coffee in Spain, you can still find the traditional *torrefacto,* natural roast, or *mezcla* (*torrefacto* blended with natural roast) served and sold in traditional cafés and grocery stores across the country.

A tiled wall at Café Central, Málaga, promises coffee to suit all tastes, from the solo, a regular black coffee, to the no me lo pongo. With a touch of humor, the last is an empty glass—literally "no more for me, please."

TOMA CAFÉ
TOMA
CAFES & ESPRESSOS
COLD BREW

LA MARZOCCO

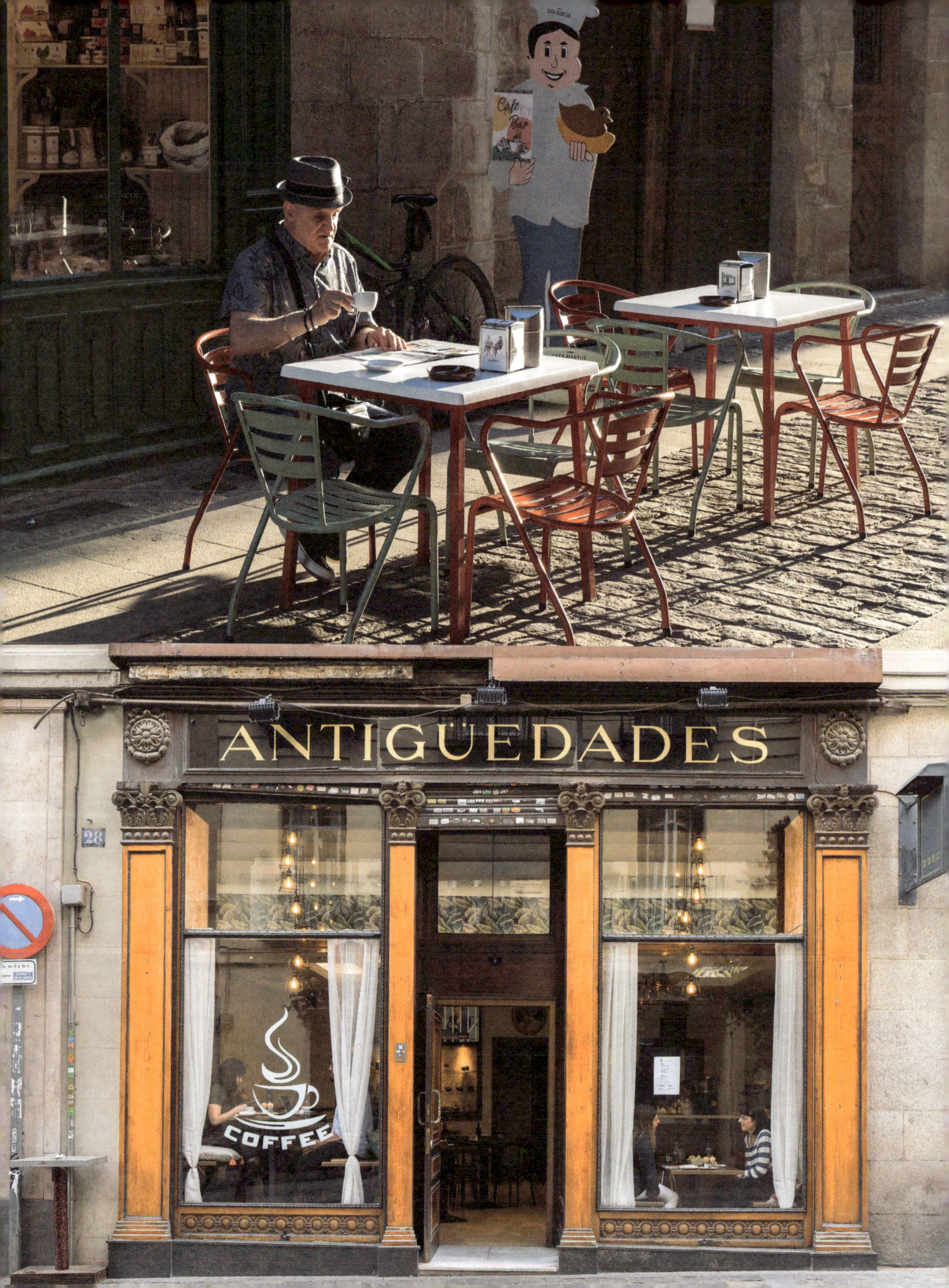
Café
Bar
ANTIGÜEDADES
28
COFFEE

Carajillo

SERVES 1

Coffee with Brandy

While the true origin of the *carajillo* is not known, the folk story goes that Spanish troops would add brandy to their coffee for liquid courage (*el coraje*). This coffee cocktail is now common across the Spanish-speaking world, and while the standard uses brandy, others use whisky, cognac, rum, anisette, or Licor 43.

60 ml (2 fl oz) brandy

2–3 coffee beans

1 tsp sugar

120 ml (4 fl oz) espresso or freshly brewed black coffee

In a small metal milk pitcher, combine the brandy, coffee beans, and sugar. Preferably using a long-reach lighter, very carefully set the brandy mixture alight (see Notes, below). After 5–8 seconds, place a saucer over the top of the pitcher to extinguish the flame, then pour into a serving glass.

Pour the coffee over the brandy, and mix before serving.

Notes:

We can't recommend to the inexperienced to set alcohol on fire at home, but if you do plan to try it, watch some videos online first to help you do it safely. With the small amount of alcohol used for one serving, the flame might be invisible, or close to it. The recipe varies all over the Spanish-speaking world. Try adding a small piece of cinnamon stick or a bit of lemon peel before setting the brandy alight—or, vary the liquor you use.

Cremat

SERVES 2

Spiced Coffee and Rum

A traditional drink of Catalonia, the alcoholic *cremat* is said to have been the drink of sailors who came back from Cuba with rum and music in their hearts. A local musical style called *habaneras* began, and these folk songs are traditionally sung while the *cremat* is set alight to burn off a little of the alcohol.

1 cup rum

1 tbsp sugar

1 small cinnamon stick

2 tbsp whole coffee beans

5-cm (2-inch) piece lemon peel

5-cm (2-inch) piece orange peel

1 cup strong coffee

You will also need:
Small heat-resistant earthenware pot, small metal pan, or small cast iron dutch oven

If you have a small heat-resistant earthenware pot, use it. Otherwise, a small metal pan or small cast iron dutch oven will do. It will need to have a fairly wide base so that the alcohol can catch on fire.

Put the rum, sugar, cinnamon, coffee beans, and citrus peels into the pot or pan. Carefully set it alight, and continually stir for 3–5 minutes to infuse the flavors and to burn off some of the alcohol.

Douse the flame by pouring over the cup of brewed coffee, stirring the coffee through until the flame disappears. Pour into serving cups once the flames are completely out.

Notes:
Take great caution with this recipe. While we can't recommend everyone to set alcohol alight in their kitchen, it's really a great drink for those comfortable with this method of cooking. If you want to give this a try, it is highly recommended that you do this outside, look up tips on flambéing safely, and make sure to use flame-resistant oven mitts and long, flameproof utensils.

Café Leche y Leche

Condensed Milk *Cortado*

Literally "coffee milk and milk," this sweet coffee drink is from Tenerife, the largest of Spain's Canary Islands. It is made by adding condensed milk to a *cortado,* a popular Spanish espresso drink with a 1:1 ratio of coffee and steamed milk (sometimes it's called a *cortado leche y leche*).

60 ml (2 fl oz) milk

2 tbsp condensed milk

60 ml (2 fl oz) espresso or strong black coffee

Foam the milk using an espresso steam wand, milk foamer, or—in a pinch—a cocktail shaker.

Pour the condensed milk into the bottom of a small glass. Pour or extract the coffee over gently so as not to disrupt the layers. Pour in the steamed milk, spooning the foam on top. Stir through before drinking.

Notes:

The *café leche y leche* is the base of a popular Canary Islands cocktail, called a *barraquito* in the South or a *zaperoco* in the North. Add a shot of Licor 43 and a chunk of lemon. Can't find Licor 43? Simply substitute another vanilla liqueur. Leave out the hot milk and just use coffee and condensed milk in a 1:1 ratio, and you've mastered another Spanish classic, the *café bombón,* hailing from Valencia.

Coffee, Rum, and Revolution

1791, Saint-Domingue: 89 percent of the population were enslaved African people, many of whom worked on sugar and coffee plantations. Realizing the power in numbers, they rebelled, destroying the plantations and forging a path towards the world's first Black-led republic: Haiti.

The Caribbean archipelago comprises an area of over a million square miles, generally taken to include 13 independent states and 17 dependent territories. After Christopher Columbus' 1492 voyage opened a sea route between Europe and the Americas, colonizers from Spain, Britain, the Netherlands, and France brought about immense changes in the region.

Coffee was introduced into the Caribbean in the early 1700s by the French and the Dutch. The trees were planted on the islands of Martinique and Saint-Domingue (the French colony on the island of Hispaniola, now Haiti and the Dominican Republic) and mainland Suriname. The common origin myth of coffee in the Americas tells of a French naval officer, Gabriel de Clieu, who transported a seedling over a long sea voyage to the French Colony of Martinique circa 1720.

Only 50 years later, Martinique was home to more than 18 million coffee trees, many of which were said to be propagated from de Clieu's seedling. These first few coffee plants in Martinique were the progenitors of the majority of the original coffee trees that spread across the Caribbean and South and Central America. Coffee is thought to have, however, arrived slightly earlier in Saint-Domingue and Suriname, and coffee fever had already begun to spread in the Americas before de Clieu reached Martinique with a live plant.

Colonial exploitation transformed the Caribbean, from the decimation of indigenous populations to the introduction of the slave trade, and the institution of a plantation economy. Historians debate exactly how many Africans were brought to the Americas via the transatlantic slave trade, up until the practice was outlawed in the nineteenth century. What is certain is that many millions arrived in the Caribbean, many of them to work on sugar or coffee plantations.

By 1791, Saint-Domingue was the most profitable colony in the Americas; the tiny island produced half the world's coffee and 40 percent of its sugar. Eighty-nine percent of the island's population were enslaved people. The same year, the enslaved rebelled, destroying the plantations and estates and defeating the French. Called the Haitian Revolution, it led to the abolishment of slavery in all French territories and went down in history as the single most successful slave rebellion.

After the destruction of their plantations, the defeated French plantation owners fled and migrated to Cuba, Jamaica, Louisiana, and Puerto Rico, bringing their skills and knowledge, and bolstering these growing coffee industries. While the island of Hispaniola never fully regained its status as a leading global coffee producer, Haiti and the Dominican Republic are now the largest coffee producers in the Caribbean today. The majority of coffee farms are run by smallholder farmers.

At the beginning of the nineteenth century, Cuba became a major coffee producer. Production peaked and waned over the next two centuries, with Cuban farmers affected by trade embargoes, duties imposed by trading partners, hurricanes, the Cuban Revolution, →

CAFÉ
AHORRANDO
SEGUIMOS EN COMBATE
El Dandy
Cafe expreso
Cafe cortado
Cafe americano
Cafe con Leche
Cafe Capuccino
Cafe Frio
Cafe Dandy
Té
Leche c/chocolate
Limonada
Jugo Fresco
Refresco Nacional
Agua Natural
Agua con Gas
Cerveza
Mojito Virgen
10% Servicio

5
KōNO
COFFEE SYPHON
MADE IN JAPAN
KōNO
MARLEY
COFFEE

→ the collapse of the Soviet Union (a main trading partner), and declining global coffee prices. Throughout the ups and downs, the Cuban love of drinking coffee has endured. In the years when production waned, Cuba imported coffee for domestic consumption.

On the sugar plantations of the Caribbean, it was discovered that molasses, a by-product of sugar refining, could be fermented and distilled. Sugarcane rum eventually became a staple in the region, and in Jamaica particularly, rum and coffee have enjoyed a long romance.

Since the Cuban Missile Crisis in 1962, Cuba has been plagued by food insecurity, and has rationed food at subsidized prices. Coffee is part of the food ration, and further supplies can either be bought on the black market or, if the means allow, from the free market at very high prices. Much of the coffee rations are blended with chickpeas or chicory to stretch the supply.

Despite the scarcities, Cuban coffee culture runs deep. While the traditional coffee-brewing method is the cloth filter used across Latin America, Cubans now like to brew in a *cafetera* (stovetop espresso maker, *moka* pot, or a *greca* in other parts of the Caribbean) or drink espresso. The Cuban's favorite coffee, the *cafecito* (known as café cubano, Cuban coffee, outside of Cuba) is made by whipping a little espresso and brown sugar into a caramel-colored foam, called *espuma*. This rises to the top of the cup as the rest of the coffee is poured in. Because coffee has long been expensive and hard to buy in volume, at times the used coffee grounds from hotels and cafés were sold to the *puestos de cafés* (coffee stalls) and cheaper establishments, who used it to make *café de recuelo* (twice-strained coffee).

Jamaica is renowned for coffee grown in the Blue Mountain region, declared by Ian Fleming's hero James Bond as "the most delicious coffee in the world." For decades, this coffee has been revered for its flavor and low bitterness. In the 1980s, however, the government realized that more Blue Mountain coffee was being sold than was actually being produced. To prevent their prized coffee's reputation from being tarnished irreparably, the government pushed for Blue Mountain coffee to be recognized internationally as a product of protected geographical indication (PGI).

Despite the scarcities, Cuban coffee culture runs deep. While the traditional coffee-brewing method is the cloth filter used across Latin America, Cubans now like to brew in a *cafetera* or drink espresso.

Now, 100 percent Blue Mountain coffee has to go through stringent protocols, ensuring that the coffee is of a particular quality from a particular source. Producers have spent several decades building the Blue Mountain brand, exporting certified coffee in signature wooden barrels, and registering trademarks in more than 50 countries. Blue Mountain coffee had built itself a reputation for traceable, single-origin, quality coffee before those traits became trendy in specialty coffee. Japan, a coffee market always looking for quality, has been a dedicated buyer since the 1970s, purchasing over 80 percent of all Jamaican coffee.

On the sugar plantations of the Caribbean, it was discovered that molasses, a by-product of sugar refining, could be fermented and distilled. Sugarcane rum eventually became a staple in the region, and in Jamaica particularly, rum and coffee have enjoyed a long romance. Although now produced in Italy, the →

→ coffee-vanilla liqueur Tia Maria was originally made in Jamaica, using local coffee and Jamaican rum.

In many countries in Latin America, coffee is traditionally brewed in a cloth filter sock and sweetened with sugar. There are many slight variations to the filter method. Some cloth filters sit in wooden frames, like the *chorreador* in Costa Rica; others sit a filter over a brewing pot, as with the *colador de café* in Mexico, Puerto Rico, and the Dominican Republic. In the Dominican Republic, there is the confusingly named *medio pollo* (half chicken), which is an espresso with a little milk.

In Haiti and in some other Latin American countries, coffee is sometimes roasted and then coated with sugar. This is a method used in a number of countries, from Spain through to Southeast Asia, to add a layer of flavor, preserve the beans from oxidation, or to add volume to the valuable ingredient.

(Below) Marley Coffee is one of several farms growing coffee in the Blue Mountains of Jamaica. (Page 134) A Caribbean man makes a slow brew using an all-glass KONO siphon vacuum coffee maker.

RINCÓN
DEL
CAFÉ
CAFE

CAFETERÍA
DOÑA FINA
CAFETERÍA
DOÑA FINA

Esencia de Café

SERVES 2–4

Coffee Essence

In Latin America and across the Caribbean, many people make this simple coffee concentrate to keep on hand, mixing a few spoonfuls into hot (or cold) water or milk, like a DIY instant coffee. It is often placed on a table so the coffee drinker can make the drink as strong or as weak as they like.

5 heaping tbsp light-
to medium-roast coffee
Grind size: fine

1 cup hot water (90°C/194°F)

You will also need:
Metal cafetera gota a gota *(drop-by-drop coffee maker)* (see Notes, below), *wooden stirrer*

Place the coffee into the filter and tap lightly to level out the grounds. If your filter has a tamper insert, set this in place, lightly press down and pour enough of the water over to saturate the grounds. If not, pour enough in to saturate and use a wooden stirrer to stir until the water filters through.

Then, pour the rest of the water over the coffee in concentric circles, slowly and steadily. Leave it to filter through. It should be ground finely enough that it takes a couple of minutes to fully extract. The extraction should be thick, syrupy, and strong. If it is not, try grinding the coffee more finely.

You can use a few tablespoons of the extraction in hot or cold water or milk, adjusting to your preferred strength.

Store leftovers in a clean, airtight jar in the refrigerator. It lasts at least a week, so you could make a larger batch for quick and easy DIY coffee.

Notes:

If you don't have a metal *cafetera gota a gota* (pictured on page 138), or a Vietnamese or South Indian-style metal filter (which is a similar design), you can use any drip brewer. This is best made with a light-roast specialty-grade coffee. You can also add sugar into the ground coffee before extracting to make the coffee essence sweet. Some people simply mix a thick paste of instant coffee and water, or boil coffee down until it has reduced to a thick essence.

The

Cafecito

Cuban Coffee

Before the *cafetera* (stovetop espresso maker), the strong, small, and sweet *cafecito* (known elsewhere as *café cubano*) was made by boiling water, sugar, and coffee and filtering it through a *colador* (cloth filter). Today in Cuba, ground dark-roasted beans are brewed in a *cafetera* or espresso machine, the first few drops whisked with sugar to create a thick *espuma* (foam).

1 small cup dark-roast coffee made with a cafetera *(see method, page 140), or, a double espresso (see method, page 36)*

1 tsp demerara sugar

Put the sugar in your serving cup.

If using a *cafetera* (stovetop espresso maker), pour the first ½ tsp of coffee that reaches the top chamber over the sugar in the cup and return the *cafetera* to the heat to continue brewing. If using espresso, extract the first couple of drips over the sugar in the cup, then extract the remainder into a (prewarmed) small vessel that you can pour from.

Using a spoon or a small whisk, vigorously beat the sugar and coffee into a paste, continuing until slightly foamed—this is your *espuma*.

When the rest of your coffee is done extracting, pour it carefully into the *espuma* so that, when the cup is full, the *espuma* is largely sitting on top of your drink.

If the sugar paste was not beaten until foamy, or too little liquid was used, it can sit heavily at the bottom of the cup. If this seems to be happening, stop pouring and whisk again with the extra liquid.

Notes:

You can use ordinary cane sugar instead, but demerara sugar adds a distinct molasses flavor. If you like it with milk, you can either top it up with warmed milk to taste or add a dash of evaporated milk. Beat the sugar for longer than you think—it takes a while to foam.

Caffeine's Highs and Lows in Brazil

1930s, São Paulo: to stop the risk of global price collapse caused by oversupply, the government purchased coffee from farmers, dumping it at sea, burning it, or using it to power trains and small towns.

Brazil is the world's largest coffee producer, and it has held this position for the majority of the last 150 years. Brazil's connection with coffee is said to have begun when one Francisco de Melo Palheta was dispatched to French Guiana to resolve a border dispute, smuggling out some coffee plants on his return to Brazil in 1727. The story goes that he began a romantic affiliation with the French governor's wife, who gifted him a large bouquet upon his departure, in which the coffee seeds were hidden.

This origin legend is likely exaggerated (or fabricated entirely), but coffee production in Brazil certainly began its ascent around this time, with the country becoming the world's leading producer over the following decades. By 1850, Brazil was producing more than half the world's coffee; by the early twentieth century, it produced almost five times as much as the rest of the world combined.

The initial labor force for Brazil's large *fazendas* (coffee plantations) were enslaved Africans, brought to Brazil through the transatlantic slave trade. An estimated 4–5 million Africans were brought to Brazil before slavery was abolished in 1888, many of whom were sent to work on plantations.

After the abolition of slavery, the planter class (a wealthy elite who had largely built their fortunes owning plantations run by enslaved people) turned to immigrant labor, primarily from Europe. In many cases, these immigrants were barely treated better than the enslaved people of a few decades before. Because of the poor working conditions on the plantations, Italy banned the Brazilian government from subsidizing immigration for agricultural workers. Consequently, Brazil began to look elsewhere for labor for the *fazendas.*

In early twentieth-century Japan, overpopulation had become a concern. The cause was a combination of natural disasters, war, a desire to become self-sufficient, and population growth, exacerbated by the return of military personnel from overseas. These changes brought about poverty, especially amongst rural agricultural workers. Japan was looking for ways to solve its population problem, Brazil's coffee farms needed workers, so the two governments came to an agreement. Many of the resulting "coffee immigrants" from Japan eventually settled in Brazil. To this day, Brazil has the largest population of people of Japanese descent outside of Japan.

Brazil's production levels were so high that it led to a global reduction in the price of coffee, which made coffee more affordable for consumers. As a result, up until the late 1800s, global demand continued to increase. At the dawn of the new century, however, Brazil's consistently increasing production finally outpaced demand, and coffee prices fell to at or below the cost of production.

In 1906, disaster was imminent—production volume was due to almost double from the previous harvest following a bumper crop. The state of São Paulo stepped in with a valorization plan: the government would purchase that year's coffee harvest at a reasonable price and hold it until prices increased, →

Quitanda
RESTAURANTE BAR
AQUI TEM
FARMÁCIA
POPULAR
Praia
SKOL
SKOL

O MELHOR QUE APARECEU
F. ROXINHO NOVO
12,00 KILO
AMENDOIM
CAVALO BRANCO
NOVO
R$ 14,00 Kg
ARROZ
NOVO
R$ 20,00 Kg
PARÁ NOVA
R$ 25,00 Kg
AVELÃ
NOVA
R$ 38,00 Kg
CAFÉ
Confetti
Oggi Sposi

→ only releasing enough coffee to meet world demand. This stopped the coffee price from dropping further, and valorization became key to the government's coffee policies in the decades to come.

In Brazil, traditional coffee is brewed simply and preferred without the addition of flavorings or creamer. If anything, milk will be added for a *café com leite*, popular at breakfast time.

Ultimately, this policy just kicked the problem further down the road—coffee production continued to expand, and other countries interpreted what they saw as Brazil's reduction in output as an opportunity to increase theirs. The continued oversupply came to a head during the Great Depression, when a world coffee crisis took hold. The Brazilian government continued to purchase farmers' crops when possible. To help prevent the price collapse of the country's primary export, surplus stocks were burned, dumped in the sea, or compressed into bricks to power trains. The towns of Niterói and Santos also used excess coffee to produce power for household consumption—low-grade coffee turned into bricks mixed with tar was cheaper than coal at the time.

In many other coffee-producing regions around the world, a majority of the homegrown crop was reserved for export, leaving little for locals and farmers to consume themselves. In Brazil, the high production volumes meant that there was enough coffee to allow domestic consumption to grow too, although much of the coffee reserved for the domestic market was of the lowest quality. Today, Brazil is the only coffee-producing country that is also a high-level consuming country.

In the mid-1800s, coffee was sometimes prepared with garlic, which was believed to cure drunkenness or illness. Today, the most-popular drink is the *cafézinho* (Portuguese for small coffee). On coffee plantations, fresh coffee would be finely ground, brewed, and filtered through a cloth to produce a very strong brew, and today it's often enjoyed with lots of sugar.

The *cafézinho* is a key part of Brazilian hospitality—you will be welcomed with one wherever you visit, and it will often be offered free or inexpensively at restaurants or gas stations. In the larger cities, trays of coffee will be available in offices, where workers can break up the monotony of the day by coming together for a quick caffeine boost. Coffee is so important that coffee servers will sometimes be credited in Brazilian movies—and the word for breakfast in Brazilian Portuguese is *café da manhã*, literally, morning coffee.

Coffee bars serve *cafézinho* to standing customers—many cups are drunk over the course of a day, so coffee is not usually a sit-down affair. These stand-up bars also usually serve shots of *cachaça*, a Brazilian sugarcane spirit. *Pão de queijo* (tapioca and cheese mini snack breads) are often served on the side.

The *cafézinho* is small and very strong, but you can also get a regular black coffee called a *café puro*. In Brazil, traditional coffee is brewed simply and preferred without the addition of flavorings or creamer. If anything, milk will be added for a *café com leite*, popular at breakfast time. This is usually half hot milk and half strong coffee, but for just a drop of milk, you can also ask for the *café pingado* (from the Portuguese word for "drop," *pingo*).

With Brazil currently ranking as the second-largest coffee consumer in the world, the drink plays an integral role in day-to-day life. It is frequently drunk on the go and commonly made using a cloth filter (pictured opposite, bottom).

Panificadora Pão de Mel
Contatos
9170-3234
9358-9276

Cafézinho

SERVES 1

Small Black Coffee

Small, strong, and heavily sweetened, this quickly drunk pick-me-up is a frequent punctuation to the average Brazilian's day. A cloth filter is used to brew finely-ground fresh coffee, resulting in a rich, full-bodied cup with an excellent mouthfeel.

180 ml (6 fl oz) water

20 g (4 level tbsp) coffee
Grind size: fine

1 tsp sugar

Pão de queijo, *for serving*

You will also need:

Cloth filter and drip stand
(see Notes, below)

If this is the first time you are using your cloth filter, rinse it well and place it over the drip stand. Place your serving cup below to capture the coffee.

Bring the water and sugar to just below a boil in a small saucepan, stirring to dissolve the sugar. Reduce the heat to low, add the ground coffee, then stir for 15 seconds. Remove from the heat.

Pour the coffee into the filter. If you don't have a drip stand, you can hold the cloth filter by the handle as the brew filters through.

If you prefer it *com leite* (with milk), add hot milk to taste. Best served with *pão de queijo* (Brazilian tapioca cheese bread).

Notes:

Cloth filters, while filtering out many small particles, generally allow more coffee oils to come through than paper filters do. This results in a different flavor and experience than you get from regular filter coffee. When using a cloth filter, it's important to rinse in water (no soap!) after every use and then keep it wet between brews. Submerge it in water and store it in the refrigerator if you plan to use it frequently, or put it in the freezer while it's still damp.

Fincas, Farms, and Niche Markets in Mexico

Early 1900s, Mexican Revolution: women called *soldaderas* or *adelitas* took on a range of active and support roles in the Mexican army. Some ran camp kitchens, brewing pots of *café de olla* to fuel the soldiers on the front line.

A pioneer in organically produced coffee, Mexico is one of the world's largest certified-organic coffee exporters. Most of the coffee grown in Mexico is shade-grown *arabica,* and the majority of coffee farms are small and family-owned, comprising less than two hectares (five acres).

It hasn't always been this way, though. Mexico was introduced to coffee around the end of the eighteenth century. Commercial coffee production was initially centered in the southern state of Veracruz but soon spread to the mountains of nearby Chiapas, Oaxaca, and Puebla, where it was grown by indigenous farmers alongside subsistence crops.

From the 1850s, land privatization laws allowed wealthy Mexicans and elites from abroad to register ownership of what they claimed was unowned land, pushing many subsistence farmers off their communally held lands and forcing them into exploitative work on the large coffee plantations (*fincas*) they built. Some smallholders kept up production, but the *fincas* dominated many regions.

After the Mexican Revolution (1910–20), many of these *fincas* were broken up through agrarian reforms, and the land was granted to the indigenous and peasant communities to use. A significant portion of these land parcels had well-established coffee trees, so *campesinos* (peasant farmers) continued to farm the land and harvest the coffee.

The Instituto Mexicano del Café (Mexican Coffee Institute) was formed in 1958 to support coffee cultivation and promotion. The Coffee Institute provided these smallholder farmers, as well as their larger-scale counterparts, with technical assistance, loans, subsidized transport, marketing, and processing. It also helped to ensure that export prices were high and stable. Other aims were to secure more land for coffee growing and to intensify production on land already used to grow coffee. As a result, coffee production increased.

In 1982, the Mexican debt crisis caused a gradual pulling-back of support for small farmers. Several years later, the Mexican Coffee Institute folded, leaving a massive gap that was quickly filled by the predatory *coyotes.* Isolated farmers without transport were left with no option but to take whatever the *coyotes* would pay because they could not get their coffee to market on their own. In addition, the majority of Mexican coffee producers were from indigenous communities and did not speak Spanish, making it practically impossible for them to participate in international coffee trade on their own. The *coyotes* have been known to engage in exploitative practices such as offering food rather than proper payment for coffee.

Gradually, other intermediaries stepped in or were created by the producers themselves, including unions, cooperatives, and export organizations, in an attempt to fill the void the Coffee Institute had left. Mexican smallholder coffee farmers continue to struggle with global low prices and other difficulties in the trade sector. →

CENAS
CAFE
PASTELES
FRAPPECHINOS
FARMACIA COYOACAN
PERFUMERIA REGALOS JUGUETES KODAK
COYOACAN
Coca-Cola
PALETAS
PALETAS
HELADOS

Café

→ To help combat some of these issues, many Mexican coffee farmers have turned to niche coffee markets for their exported coffee, such as organic and fair trade, to try to obtain a better price.

The *café de olla* (pot coffee) is brewed in a similar way to traditional cacao, simmered in an earthenware pot with *piloncillo* (unrefined sugar). The folk legend of *café de olla* is that it fueled the Mexican Revolution, brewed for soldiers on the front line.

Farmers are also struggling with climate change and coffee rust disease, which is caused by the fungus *Hemileia vastatrix*, known as *la roya* in Spanish. Because many Mexican farmers are involved in the organic production of *arabica*, they are highly susceptible to coffee rust, which can cause the loss of coffee trees and sometimes entire farms. Coffee trees take many years to bear fruit, so the replanting of devastated trees is sometimes not an option for smallholder farmers. Where possible, Mexican farmers are trying to replant with rust-resistant varieties.

In Mexico, coffee is traditionally brewed in a similar way to other Latin American countries—steeped and then filtered through a cloth sock called a *colador de tela*. While espresso is also drunk in Mexico, this steeped filter coffee is what you usually get at *mercados* (open-air markets) or *panaderías* (bakeries), served black or with hot milk, with a side of *pan dulce* (sweet bread). Coffee beans are sometimes roasted in sugar in Mexico and other parts of Latin America, similar to the *torrefacto* roast in Spain (see page 121) or the *kopi* roast in Singapore (see page 204) and Malaysia. In Veracruz, the traditional *café lechero* (milk coffee) is made by holding metal kettles filled with hot milk high over a glass that holds a little coffee and pouring the milk in a slow, steady stream. The height of the pour aerates the milk and coffee, creating froth.

Cacao has been consumed as a drink in ancient Mesoamerica for thousands of years. Cinnamon, not native to Mexico, was introduced much later but is now a frequent addition to many traditional recipes, including coffee. The *café de olla* (pot coffee) is brewed in a similar way to traditional cacao, simmered in an earthenware pot with *piloncillo* (unrefined sugar). The folk legend of *café de olla* is that it fueled the Mexican Revolution, brewed for soldiers on the front line.

Because many Mexican farmers are involved in the organic production of arabica, they are highly susceptible to coffee rust, which can cause the loss of coffee trees and sometimes entire farms.

The alcoholic *carajillo*, common in many Spanish-speaking countries, is very popular in Mexico, too. Traditionally made with coffee and brandy, in Mexico it is often made with Licor 43: a Spanish liqueur flavored with citrus, vanilla, and a number of secret herbs and spices.

In recent years, urban Mexican cafés have started serving Americanos, espressos, and cappuccinos, but you will still find waiters pacing the floors at Gran Café de la Parroquia in Veracruz, dispensing café lechero from metal kettles.

DONAS
galletas
strudel
CAFÉ
espresso
cappuccino
frappuccino

LA VENTANA
expendio de café
Café Orgánico
de Chiapas

Coffee Liqueur

Coffee Cocktail

This recipe blends sugarcane rum with strong coffee and vanilla, and is delicious drunk on its own. In Veracruz, Mexico, a recipe for coffee blended with rum has been immortalized by the famous commercial liqueur, Kahlúa.

1 cup sugar

1 cup strong hot coffee

1 vanilla bean

2 cups sugarcane rum (see Notes, below)

You will also need:
1 clean 750 ml (25 fl oz) glass bottle with a resealable cap, such as a liqueur bottle

Put the sugar into a large pitcher, and pour the hot coffee over. Stir until completely dissolved. Scrape the seeds from the vanilla bean into the coffee, stir, and let cool.

Place a funnel in the top of the bottle, and pour the rum into it. Add the scraped vanilla bean to the bottle, too.

Once the coffee and sugar mixture is cool, pour it into the bottle, seal, and leave to infuse in a cool, dark place for 3–4 weeks.

Notes:
You can use either light, dark, or spiced rum according to your preference. Dark rum will add a molasses flavor. If you want to increase that caramel flavor, you could also use brown sugar instead of ordinary sugar.

Café de Olla

SERVES 3–4

Cinnamon Coffee

This traditional coffee is said to date back to the Mexican Revolution, when it was prepared for soldiers on the front line. It is brewed in a signature earthenware pot, called a *café de olla* (which gives this drink its name), then spiced with cinnamon and sweetened with *piloncillo,* an unrefined cane sugar, which helps counter the bitterness caused by boiling the coffee beans.

3 cups water

1 Mexican cinnamon stick

60–100 g (2–3 ½ oz) piloncillo (see Notes, below)

6 level tbsp dark-roast coffee
Grind size: medium coarse

Pan dulce, *for serving*

You will also need:
Lead-free, stove-safe earthenware pot (see Notes, below), *filter or strainer*

Place the water, cinnamon stick, and 60 g *piloncillo* (about one-quarter of a cone) into the pot set over a high heat. Bring up to a boil, and let the *piloncillo* melt into the water. Carefully taste a little of the brew and add extra *piloncillo* if you'd like it sweeter.

Turn down the heat and simmer for 10 minutes, then turn off the heat. Let cool for 2 minutes. Add the ground coffee, and stir through. Let steep for 5 minutes.

Using a filter, a fine-mesh sieve, or a cheesecloth-lined regular sieve, ladle the coffee into a prewarmed serving pitcher, or directly into your cup.

Serve with freshly baked *pan dulce* (sweet bread).

Notes:
In Mexico, some coffee is coated with sugar during the roasting process. This adds bitterness and intensity to the coffee, so if you are using a natural roast, you'll want to try and find a dark roast to simulate this flavor. The earthenware pot is said to contribute to the flavor, but if you don't have one, you can use a regular pot or saucepan. The *piloncillo* is very important for the molasses flavor, but if you can't find *piloncillo*, you can substitute it with dark brown sugar—just reduce the amount a little.

From Volcanoes to Vanilla Plantations in Polynesia

1825, Mānoa Valley, Hawai'i: the governor of O'ahu, Chief Boki, returns from a state trip to London via Brazil, where he collected coffee seedlings to begin Hawai'i's first coffee orchard.

Thousands of inhabited islands are scattered across the Pacific Ocean. While many are independent nations, they are grouped according to proximity and/or culture into Micronesia, Melanesia, and Polynesia. The Polynesian Triangle includes more than 1,000 islands whose peoples share some commonality in language, culture, and traditions and are collectively known as Polynesians. Generally accepted to include Hawai'i, New Zealand, Sāmoa, Tonga, Tahiti, and other islands, many fall within what's known as the bean belt, a region 25 degrees north and 30 degrees south of the equator with an ideal climate for growing coffee.

While many of the islands in Polynesia grow coffee, of particular note is Hawai'i. The first coffee was planted on the islands in the early 1800s, which led to the development of a now world-famous coffee cultivation. By the 1840s, the government accepted payment of land taxes in coffee. *Kope* (coffee) is now grown on all the major Hawaiian islands, but the name of Kona, a district on the Big Island of Hawai'i, has become synonymous with quality coffee worldwide. Kona coffee, grown on the slopes of volcanoes, often demands the highest prices.

Kona coffee is usually handpicked. That, in combination with limited land for coffee growing compared to, say, Brazil, means that there's not a lot of Kona coffee available. It is rare to see Kona or other Hawaiian-grown coffees for sale outside Hawai'i. Another reason for this is because Hawai'i is a U.S. state, so coffee farmworkers are paid the American minimum wage. The higher wages and costs result in a coffee that is more expensive than that grown elsewhere—green (unroasted) coffee from Hawai'i average at around $20 per pound, while the average price for specialty green coffee was between $1.90–$3.50 per pound in 2020. These comparisons reveal the true cost of coffee-farm labor and help to highlight the potential inequalities in the wages that workers may be paid in other coffee-producing countries.

The Kona coffee harvest usually begins around November, and it has been celebrated annually since 1970 with the Kona Coffee Culture Festival. A Miss Kona Coffee is crowned in a scholarship pageant, during which professional judges also blind-taste and score (a process called cupping, see page 262) Kona coffee from a number of local producers.

Macadamia nuts, native to Australia, were introduced to Hawai'i in the 1800s and were quickly adopted into Hawaiian cuisine. Requiring similar growing conditions to coffee, these two crops were often grown in the same farms and regions. Now you can easily find macadamia-flavored coffee throughout the islands. Coffee is often used in cooking and baking, too—you'll find locally grown coffee in both sweet and savory dishes.

Located much further south than other islands in Polynesia, New Zealand has never been a key area for →

COFFEES OF HAWAI'I

→ coffee cultivation because of its cooler climate. However, the *Coprosma* genus of flowering plants, native to New Zealand and other Pacific Islands, are in the same taxonomic family as *Coffea rubiaceae*. While this does not in and of itself infer a close relationship (there are more than 6,500 species in the *rubiaceae* family), early European settlers in New Zealand quickly noticed the similarity between the cherries produced by *Coprosma* and those produced by *Coffea*.

> Like macadamia in Hawai'i, vanilla thrived in similar environmental conditions to coffee, so both crops came to be grown in the same places. It was only a matter of time before Tahitians began to add a vanilla pod to their coffee pot.

J. C. Crawford, a keen amateur geologist and agriculturalist, moved from Britain to Australia and New Zealand in the late 1830s. He shared a paper with the Wellington Philosophical Society in 1877, referring to a species of *Coprosma* known in Māori as *karamū*. His paper leads with the statement that coffee of fine flavor has been produced from the beans of the *karamū*, and goes on to detail his experiments with another species of *Coprosma*, called *taupata* in Māori. He harvested, removed the pulp, and roasted the beans, noting that, "when roasted and ground, they have a splendid coffee aroma, and when made into coffee, the result seems to be thoroughly satisfactory." The Māori consumed these indigenous plants, too, but not in the same way: the berries were eaten, or they were used in *rongoā*, Māori traditional medicine.

Coffee is also cultivated in French Polynesia. Five groups of islands are part of this overseas collectivity of France, which was made a French protectorate in the 1800s. Around the same time, the French introduced vanilla to the islands, which was to become a major export crop for Tahiti.

> While many of the islands in Polynesia grow coffee, of particular note is Hawai'i. The first coffee was planted on the islands in the early 1800s, which led to the development of a now world-famous coffee cultivation.

Like macadamia in Hawai'i, vanilla thrived in similar environmental conditions to coffee, so both crops came to be grown in the same places. It was only a matter of time before Tahitians began to add a vanilla pod to their coffee pot. Today, coffee is often flavored with vanilla across French Polynesia, topped off with fresh coconut cream (and sometimes a little local Tahitian honey).

(Opposite) Hawai'i's Kauai Coffee iconic hula girl rises in the steam of a freshly poured cup of coffee, much like a genie from a lamp. "Some coffee for you?" asks the byline.

GRANDMA'
COFFEE HOUSE
COFFEE

Coconut Vanilla Coffee

Vanilla and coffee were introduced to French Polynesia during the nineteenth century. Both have been grown for export ever since to varying degrees, and the availability of coffee, vanilla, and coconut in these Pacific Islands has influenced the local cuisine.

1 vanilla bean

1 × 400 ml (13.5 fl oz) can unsweetened coconut milk

3 tbsp honey

1 cup black coffee per serving

Cut open the vanilla bean and scrape the seeds into a small saucepan. Add the scraped vanilla bean to the pan too. Pour in the coconut milk, and bring to a low simmer over a gentle heat.

Use a whisk to distribute the vanilla seeds evenly throughout the milk, and after 2–3 minutes, remove from the heat, stir the honey through, and leave to cool.

Brew a cup of black coffee, then add a little vanilla coconut milk to taste. Depending on your brand of coconut milk, you might find that the fat begins to separate. To prevent separation, you can whizz the mixture in a blender for a few minutes to emulsify and froth the drink.

Any leftover vanilla coconut milk can be stored in a clean sealed jar (with the vanilla bean left inside) in the refrigerator for a few days.

Notes:

This recipe makes an easy-to-use vanilla coconut milk that can be added to any coffee, but you could also split open a vanilla bean and drop it into a French press with the coffee. Then, after you brew as normal, pour in a little coconut milk or cream when you serve, to taste. You won't need sugar in this coffee, but if you do have a sweet tooth, add some local honey, as the Tahitians do.

Kodawari, Kissaten, and Coffee Culture in Japan

1888, Tokyo: Japan's first *kissaten* (traditional coffeehouse) opened. Over the following century, *kissaten* dedicated to specialized brewing would win Japan an international reputation for quality coffee.

When coffee first arrived in Japan around 1700, it did not immediately suit local tastes. It was favored by Dutch merchants and traders headquartered in Nagasaki and took hold only gradually in Japanese society, originally for medicinal purposes, or as a foreign curiosity. 大田 南畝 Ōta Nanpo, a revered poet born in 1749, notoriously said, "I was recommended *Kauhii* (coffee) on a red-haired (Dutch) boat. Beans are roasted black and powdered, and white sugar is added. It smells burnt and I can't stand the taste."

Merry White, professor of anthropology at Boston University in the United States, details in *Coffee Life in Japan* that after the 1860s, during the Meiji era (1868–1912), coffee-drinking made its way to the countryside: there, *koohiito,* a ball of ground coffee and sugar (sometimes offered to children as a treat) was a crude type of instant coffee that could be dropped into hot water and easily drunk.

Coffee consumption really took hold in the early 1900s. The Taishō period (1912–1926) is considered Japan's jazz era. During the preceding Meiji era, elements of Western culture became trendy in Japan, but the liberal movement known as Taishō democracy further adapted Western culture into a new, Japanese modern aesthetic. During this time, 喫茶店 *kissaten* (coffee shops) began to proliferate, popularizing the モーニングセット *mōningusetto* (morning set, or morning service), a light, Western-style breakfast of tea or coffee, thick-cut toast, sometimes served with red bean jam (particularly in Nagoya), egg, and sometimes fruit, salad, and fish.

Various styles of *kissaten* emerged: while some focused on entertainment, music, serving alcohol, or even operating as erotic venues, others focused purely on the art of coffee making. A fascination with the different ways to brew coffee resulted in various *kissatens* specializing in a particular brewing method, a unique house blend, or another theme.

White and others note that the Japanese philosophy of こだわり *kodawari* (commitment) is a key part of *kissaten* culture. *Kodawari* is the striving for perfection, attention to detail, precision, and quality that the Japanese are well known for. In coffee, this approach is applied to everything from innovation, such as the manufacture of coffee equipment, to the selection of コーヒー豆 *kōhī mame* (coffee beans), and brewing methods. The quality-focused specialty-coffee movement began to take shape, and Japan is now recognized as a world leader.

Today, Japanese brewing trends, including the pour-over, siphon, and slow-drip cold-brew methods, are popular in specialty cafés outside of Japan, too. White notes that while the Japanese originally thought the espresso to be too mechanical and not handmade enough, espresso-brewing now has its own *kodawari.*

Japan's early affiliation with Brazil was key to the development of the coffee industries in both countries. In early twentieth-century Japan, overpopulation →

COFFEE JAPANESE TEA
CRAFTNUTS SOUVENIR
COFFEE
JAPANESE TEA
1800ml×8
メロン

BLACK
ONIBUS COFFEE
ONIBUS CO
Menu
FILTER
TODAY'S COFFEE 360 400
HAND DRIP 500 530
BLACK
ESPRESSO 410 510
AMERICANO 480 510
WHITE
LATTE 480 500
510 540

→ resulted in a lack of employment and consequent poverty, especially among rural agricultural workers. Japan was proactive in solving its population problem: Brazil's coffee farms needed workers after the abolition of slavery in 1888 (see page 144), so the two governments came to an agreement. Over the course of a few decades, 240,000 Japanese emigrated to Brazil, many to work on coffee plantations.

> Japan is at the forefront of quality and innovation in coffee-brewing equipment. Hario and Kalita are just two Japanese manufacturers that are renowned by baristas internationally.

Conditions in Brazil were harsh, and the immigrants were barely treated better than the enslaved workers from Africa had been. However, many Japanese worked out their contracts and eventually settled and bought their own land to farm coffee. By 1932, there were 60 million coffee trees on Japanese-owned plantations in Brazil. Brazil in turn nurtured Japan as an export market, and through various agreements, provided Japan with ample free coffee supplies. This assisted both coffee's unhindered spread throughout Japan and the proliferation of cafés. The initiative clearly worked: today, Japan is one of the largest coffee markets in the world, and Brazilian coffee is still the largest-volume coffee import.

Coffee imports and consumption fell significantly during the 1940s and 1950s because of disruption caused by the Second World War. When coffee was scarce, 大豆珈琲 *daizu kōhī,* a roasted soybean coffee, was a good substitute and was consumed from at least the 1920s. While *daizu kōhī* has largely fallen out of favor, a new wave of artisanal Japanese producers are now producing high-quality roasted soybeans, bringing about a revival of this once-popular drink.

After the 1960s, when coffee imports were resumed, Japanese coffee culture began to increase exponentially. In 1969, a Japanese company pioneered 缶コーヒー *kan kōhī* (canned coffee), which helped to popularize the beverage—it could be consumed anytime, anywhere. Canned, ready-to-drink coffee premixed with milk and sugar, is a popular version.

炭焼きコーヒー *sumiyaki kōhī* (charcoal-grilled coffee) is a traditional roasting method that has been around since the early 1900s. The green coffee beans are roasted over a charcoal heat source which gives the *sumiyaki kōhī* a distinct flavor.

Japan has developed an international reputation for cold-brew coffee, particularly for Kyoto-style coffee, which is marketed abroad. It is made using the Kyoto-style cold-brew tower which, unlike the standard immersion method of cold brew, in which coffee grounds are left to sit in cold water for many hours, water is dripped over the coffee a single drop at a time, allowing a very slow extraction.

This Kyoto-style brewer is called ダッチ コーヒー *datchi kōhī* (Dutch coffee) in Japan. Many claim that the Dutch were first to invent cold brew in the 1600s as a shelf-stable coffee for their long sea voyages, although the spectacular glass brewing towers available today are Japanese designed. These glass towers are used across Japan and in specialty cafés around the world.

The ネルドリップ *neru dorippu* (nel drip) is another Japanese drip filter, but this method uses hot water and a flannel ('nel) cloth filter. While its origins are unclear, the traditional coffee drink of Brazil, the *cafézinho,* is brewed in a similar cloth filter. Hand-brewed coffee remains popular in Japan, although, since the 1960s, the paper filter is more common than the cloth filter. Pour-over brewing methods do take →

→ time, but the spectacle and performance are an integral part of the Japanese coffee experience.

Japan is at the forefront of quality and innovation in coffee-brewing equipment. Hario and Kalita are just two Japanese manufacturers that are renowned by baristas internationally. Hario began as a heat-resistant glass manufacturer in Tokyo in 1921, and their coffee siphon (a method originally invented in Germany) was their first foray into the coffee world in 1948. Hario also took to adapting the cone-shaped dripper invented by German-based Melitta in the 1930s, with the release of the now-ubiquitous V60 conical drip brewer. With a perfect 60°-angled cone, the V60 alters the flow of water in a way that extends the contact time with the coffee. Today, the name V60 is synonymous with pour-over coffee to many coffee connoisseurs worldwide.

Epitomizing Japanese aesthetics when it comes to design, many Japanese cafés and kiosks are as highly stylized as their coffee paraphernalia—lean, pared-back interiors boast stark geometry and monochrome finishes.

BOSS
BLACK
SUNTORY
無糖・ブラック
コーヒー

日曜·休日を除く
EAVES
OFFEE
ORDER HERE
OPEN

SWS
AM9-PM9
ESPRESSO
TO GO
SANDWICHES
CRAFT BEER
SIDEWALK
STAND

ネルドリップ Neru dorippu

SERVES 1

Nel Drip

The flannel ('nel) filter traps sediment but allows more of the coffee's oils through than a paper filter would. The water temperature is lower, so less of the soluble materials that contribute to bitterness are extracted. The high ratio of coffee to water used results in a rich, syrupy, wine-like brew that can even coax flavor out of old coffee beans.

18–20 g (4 level tbsp) coffee
Grind size: medium coarse

100 g (3 ½ oz) water

You will also need:
Nel drip cloth filter and handle (see Notes, next page), *pour-over drip pot (or a carafe that your filter will sit on easily while letting the filter bag hang inside without touching the sides of the carafe), gooseneck kettle (or another vessel that will allow you to pour water in a thin, steady stream), thermometer, scales*

If this is the first use of your nel filter, immerse it in hot water for a few minutes, then gently grab the bottom tip of the filter bag and twist to wring it out.

Place the filter directly over the drip pot or carafe, (and if you have not already pre-wet it) pour hot water through it, saturating the filter and partially filling the pot to keep it warm. Pour some hot water into your serving cup. This is a low-temperature brew, so you'll want to start with warm vessels.

If you don't have a suitable carafe, you can just hold the filter by its handle over your prewarmed serving cup.

Boil some water (ideally in a gooseneck kettle), then let the water temperature drop to around 79°C (175°F)—a couple of minutes off the boil (test using a thermometer). If you didn't boil the water directly in a gooseneck kettle, pour the water into your kettle or other pouring vessel now.

Empty the water in the carafe, replace the filter, and add the ground coffee to the filter. Do not compact. Place the brewer onto the scales and press tare to set the scales to zero.

Start to drip the hot water onto the ground coffee from the center, slowly, drip by drip, until you completely saturate the coffee. When the first drip of coffee drops through into the carafe, pause. You'll see little bubbles start to form in the grounds. Wait for them to pop, leaving some small holes—this will take 45–60 seconds.

Resume, pouring very slowly but steadily up and down from the center of the coffee, until the grounds begin to bubble again. Then, move to pouring in concentric circles. Make sure the stream of water does not pour directly onto the filter but always directly on the coffee.

As the coffee grounds begin to dome up, stop, wait for them to subside a little, and begin pouring again before the bubbles completely subside. Repeat this process until the scales read 100 g (3 ½ oz). Let the brew continue to drip into the carafe, and when finished, empty out the hot water in your serving cup and pour the coffee out to serve.

After you brew, rinse the filter well in hot water. Immerse it in fresh water and keep in the refrigerator, or, if you plan to use it infrequently, put it (still wet) inside a resealable plastic bag and freeze. The next time you use it, rinse and proceed as before.

Notes:

Many *kissatens* have their own brewing ratios and methods that they have adapted for different types of beans and roasts. Start with the above recipe and experiment—it makes a very small coffee to sip, as is the fashion in a number of *kissatens.* The flannel cloth has one smooth side and one slightly fluffy side—it's said that if you brew with the fluffy side on the inside, fewer coffee oils will be extracted. Neither way is incorrect; it just depends on what you prefer in your cup. Try with the fluffy side on the outside for a deep and rich nel drip.

コーヒーサイフォン Kōhī Saifon

SERVES 1–2

Siphon Coffee

The siphon coffee brewer wasn't invented in Japan, but it did become very popular there, particularly in specialty coffee shops. Although globally the siphon brewer fell out of favor outside Japan in the 1900s, Japanese equipment manufacturers have fueled a resurgence with coffee connoisseurs around the world, who are ordering and importing high-quality Japanese siphon brewers.

25 g (5 level tbsp) coffee
Grind size: medium coarse

300 g (1 ¼ cups) water

You will also need:
Siphon brewer, thermometer, wooden stirrer

Follow manufacturer's instructions for brewer setup. Soak the filter in warm water, set in the top vessel, then pull the chain to clip at the bottom of the funnel.

Add water to the lower vessel, wiping away any drips on the outside of the brewer. Gently push the top vessel into place, and sit the brewer over an appropriate heat source. Refer to the manufacturer's instructions here.

As it heats, the water vapor expands, moving into the top vessel. When the water is fully transferred to the top chamber (it should be around 95°C (203°F) when tested with a thermometer), add the ground coffee and stir.

Turn the heat down a touch—ideally, the temperature should drop to no less than 90°C (194°F), otherwise, the coffee may drop down too quickly. Leave for 1 minute 15 seconds, then remove from the heat. Use the wooden stirrer to gently stir.

The vacuum pressure in the lower vessel will reverse—the water, now cooling, will contract. A partial vacuum of negative pressure is created, sucking the liquid back down while filtering, filling the lower vessel with brewed coffee.

Carefully remove the top vessel to pour and serve.

Notes:
Siphon brewers vary, so you may need to adapt this recipe to suit your brewer. The brewers come in different sizes, so you may need to scale the water measurement up or down, but a good ratio to stick to is 1:12–1:15 coffee to water, depending on how strong you like your coffee.

コーヒーゼリー Kōhīzerī

SERVES 3–4

Coffee Jelly

In Japan, sweet coffee jelly became a popular coffee-shop food from the *Taishō* era, when Western food and culture were in vogue. It is modeled after the set jellies of Europe, and Japan's obsession with coffee jelly continues to this day. You can find it cubed and added to iced coffee or served in a parfait with whipped cream and red bean jam.

1 tsp kanten or agar powder (see Notes, below)

3 tbsp granulated sugar

175 ml (¾ cup) water

295 ml (1¼ cups) double-strength brewed coffee (see Notes, below)

You will also need:
Small shallow glass dish or jelly mold

Mix the agar powder and ¾ cup water in a small saucepan and place over high heat. Bring to a boil, then immediately reduce to low and simmer for 5 minutes while stirring.

Add the sugar and stir through until dissolved. Remove from heat. Pour in the brewed coffee.

Pour the liquid into the dish or mold and leave to cool. Once cooled, place into the refrigerator until set.

Notes:
Both kanten and agar are setting agents made from algae, but they are made from different algae and produce slightly different results. You could also use regular gelatin. The setting strength of agar can also vary between brands. If you'd like to test yours before making this jelly, you can simmer ¼ teaspoon agar in ½ cup water for 5 minutes, and then leave to cool and set. The consistency should be such that you can slice it into cubes. If it's too soft or doesn't set, you could double the agar in the recipe. As we are diluting the coffee with the agar water, you'll need to make it double strength. If you like, you can make this with instant coffee. Replace the brewed coffee volume with water and add 2–3 tablespoons of instant coffee when you add the sugar.

アイスコーヒー Aisu kōhī

SERVES 2–3

Iced Coffee

Hot brewing extracts different flavors from the coffee beans because various compounds become soluble at different temperatures. Flash-chilling hot-brew coffee is popular in specialty coffee shops in Japan. The immediate cooling of the hot extracted coffee preserves the coffee's flavor because it prevents the oxidation that happens over a longer chilling time.

1 cup ice

30 g (6 level tbsp) light- to medium-roast coffee
Grind size: medium fine

225 g (8 oz) hot water (91–96°C/195–205°F or just off the boil)

Creamer, cream, or milk, to taste (optional)

You will also need:
Pourover or drip coffee maker, thermometer, gooseneck kettle, or something from which you can pour a thin and steady stream of water

Place the ice into the vessel your coffee will extract into, and then place your coffee maker over the top.

Place the ground coffee in the filter and shake lightly to settle the grounds. Place the brewer over a scale and press tare to reset to zero.

Pour 50 g (1¾ oz) of the water from the kettle over the coffee, allowing it to foam up slightly (this is called the bloom).

After 30 seconds, slowly begin to pour the remainder of the water over the coffee in a circular motion. Make sure that the water stream always hits the coffee, not the filter.

Let the coffee drip through onto the ice slowly. Once extracted, you can sweeten with a simple syrup and add creamer, cream, or milk, if you like.

Notes:
You can use any hot extraction method and flash chill the coffee. You can extract an espresso shot directly over ice: just swirl the cup as it's being extracted to prevent the ice from melting too quickly. If using a drip or filter recipe, reduce the water by subtracting the weight of ice. For example, if your recipe usually uses 200 g of water and you add 50 g of ice, reduce the water content to 150 g. This stops your brew from becoming diluted. If using drip methods, adjust your grind more finely to prevent under extraction. This will mean the brew takes roughly the same amount of time to extract as it would have with the original amount of water.

Boom, Bust, and a Robust Coffee Culture in Vietnam

1946, Hà Nội: an enterprising hotel bartender whipped up a creamy foam with egg yolk for coffee to replace the milk that had become scarce during the First Indochina War.

Coffee was introduced into northern Vietnam in 1857, shortly after the country came under French rule. However, production remained relatively low until the end of the Vietnam War in 1975. After almost a century of political upheaval and military conflict, the war ended with the formal reunification of North and South Vietnam under Communist rule.

During the late 1970s and 1980s, the Vietnamese government supported the growth of coffee production with favorable economic policies and subsidies. As the economy recovered, coffee growing expanded rapidly: Vietnam became the world's second-largest coffee-producing country in just a few decades.

Many farmers moved into the fertile Central Highlands region, where growing conditions are ideal for coffee cultivation. Then, in the 1990s, world coffee prices skyrocketed, which enticed even more farmers into growing coffee and reinforced Vietnam's status as a world-leading producer. In the following decade, however, boom led to bust, as a result of price volatility on the world coffee market. When prices dropped, many Vietnamese growers ended up relying on food donations to survive. The rapid growth in Vietnam's coffee production has also resulted in environmental degradation and social inequalities.

Most Vietnamese coffee producers are smallholders, so growing *robusta* rather than *arabica* was a sensible choice. *Robusta* requires less intensive maintenance than *arabica*, so costs are lower. It is also less susceptible to pests and disease, and is more climate resistant. Vietnam is now the world's largest producer of *robusta*.

Robusta's higher caffeine levels and lower sugar content are what make it less susceptible to pest damage, but these qualities result in a more intense, more bitter, and less sweet brew, too. The common *robusta* is not known in the industry for exceptional flavor, so it is often intentionally roasted dark (and sometimes blended with maize).

Coffee roasters' recipes are trade secrets so it's difficult to ascertain, but it is believed that some coffee beans are first coated in flavor-boosting ingredients, such as alcohol, fish sauce, chicken fat, butter, salt, and sugar. *Robusta*'s flavor is enhanced further when brewed with sweet and strong-flavored ingredients such as condensed milk, coconut, or ginger. *Robusta* is now the preferred style in Vietnam—on its own or blended—because most recipes have been developed with its unique flavor profile in mind.

In Sài Gòn (Ho Chi Minh City), coffee was often brewed in cloth coffee socks (similar to those used in Malaysian and Singaporean *kopitiams*, see page 207), called *cà phê vợt*. This is now considered an old-school method; most coffee shops now use a *phin*, a metal drip filter introduced by the French (*phin* derives from the French *filtre*).

While there is some disagreement about its origins, the Vietnamese drip-filter brewer is identical →

Star

→ to the *cafetière à la de Belloy* (sometimes spelled *dubelloire, Débéloire,* or *la débelloire*), which was invented in Paris sometime around 1800, and is believed to be the very first percolated coffee brewer. Jean-François Coste writes in his book *Almanach des Gourmands,* published 1805, that, "all true gourmets are eager to adopt [the use of *la cafetière Du Belloy*]." It can be fairly deduced that the French took this portable brewer with them as they began their conquest of Vietnam just a few decades later.

After a strong coffee is brewed using the *phin,* it is served to your preference as a *cà phê đen* (black coffee, to which you can add sugar), *cà phê sữa* (milk coffee, made with sweetened condensed milk), served iced (*đá*) or hot (*nóng*). In South Vietnam, a cup of coffee is often served with a cup of tea alongside.

> Even though fresh dairy is more accessible these days, the flavor of condensed milk is now inseparable from Vietnamese coffee culture. Another French introduction—yogurt—is also blended with coffee to make the *sữa chua cà phê.*

In the capital Hà Nội (Hanoi), you can still see relics of the French occupation. The streets of the French Quarter are filled with Parisian-style sidewalk coffee shops where a small, strong coffee can be enjoyed. Erica Peters notes in her book *Appetites and Aspirations in Vietnam* that many elements of French cuisine had already been adopted by the Vietnamese, from bread through to coffee, by the early 1900s. European coffee styles were adapted for local tastes—including the substitution of sweetened condensed milk for fresh milk.

The Vietnamese lacked a dairy tradition for a number of reasons: mainly, that the lack of refrigeration in the hot and humid climate made perishable milk products unfeasible. In addition, food scarcity and poverty meant that the dairy produce loved by the French was unaffordable. While condensed milk was still considered a luxury good, it was easier to preserve and could be used in smaller quantities. As a result, most milk coffee in Vietnam was made with condensed milk—a perfect partner to intense, bitter *robusta.* Even though fresh dairy is more accessible these days, the flavor of condensed milk is now inseparable from Vietnamese coffee culture. Another French introduction—yogurt—is also blended with coffee to make the *cà phê sữa chua.*

> Coffee roasters' recipes are trade secrets so it's difficult to ascertain, but it is believed that some coffee beans are first coated in flavor-boosting ingredients, such as alcohol, fish sauce, chicken fat, butter, salt, and sugar.

Then there's the *cà phê cốt dừa* (coconut coffee), usually prepared by blending coconut milk with ice and mixing it with black coffee or the *cà phê trứng* (egg coffee). The origin story of egg coffee goes that a bartender from Hà Nội was looking for a solution to dwindling milk supplies during the First Indochina War. His ingenuity led him to whip up egg yolks with a couple of other ingredients and top a black coffee with this creamy egg foam.

(Opposite, bottom) In a Vietnamese café, rows of one-cup metal drip filters jostle for shelf space with tins of coffee and condensed milk. The filter is typically placed on top of a glass before hot water is poured over the coffee grinds within.

GÓC HÀ NỘI
Little HaNoi
EGG coffee
SINCE
1940
VNPT
OPTICAB
TDJF 3220
0300 0039
147 - 148
EGG COFFEE

Cà Phê Sữa

Milk Coffee

A sweet, intense coffee brewed using a *phin* (Vietnamese coffee filter). In Hà Nội and North Vietnam, this coffee is called *cà phê nâu,* and is a little stronger and less sweet. While it's a relatively small serve, it's powerful: the high-caffeine *robusta,* ample sugar, and long brewing time pack a punch.

20 g (4 level tbsp) robusta *coffee per serving*
Grind size: fine

1–2 tbsp sweetened condensed milk

½ cup freshly boiled water per serving

You will also need:
Single-serve phin

Put the ground coffee into a single-serve *phin* (if your filter is larger, scale the recipe up); shake lightly to level.

Pour condensed milk to taste into a serving cup. Place the filter over the cup and ensure it is level.

Using the filter's press, tamp the coffee down, then leave the filter in place. Pour in a few tablespoons of freshly boiled water, then leave to sit for 30 seconds. If the coffee is fresh, it should bubble.

If the filter press lifts, gently press to level it, then top up the filter with hot water. Replace the lid.

You can brew over a glass to see how long it takes to start dripping. The first drip should take between 1 ½–2 minutes, the final between 5–6 minutes, at a rate of 1 drip every 3–5 seconds. If it drips too quickly, tamp harder (or grind more finely next time). If it drips too slowly, tamp lighter (or grind more coarsely next time).

Mix the coffee with the condensed milk and serve.

Notes:
Pour over ice for a *cà phê sữa đá* (iced coffee), which is how it is often drunk in humid Southeast Asia. You can also serve it black, dilute it with water or milk, or add coconut milk. If the coffee isn't dripping, make sure the lid hasn't formed a vacuum. If it has, remove it and dry it well before replacing. *Phin* hole sizes aren't standardized. A few coffee grounds falling through is normal. If too many fall through when you shake, try prewetting the inside of the *phin* so the grinds stick.

Cà Phê Trứng

SERVES 1

Egg Coffee

Legend has it that this sweet concoction from Hà Nội was intended to replace the French colonists' beloved cappuccino during the milk shortages of the First Indochina War. A creamy, sweet, meringue-like condensed milk custard sits on top of a dark, concentrated extraction of *robusta* coffee beans.

1 serving of cà phê đen nóng *(hot, black coffee): follow recipe for* cà phê sữa *(milk coffee; see page 196) but omit the condensed milk*

2 egg yolks

4 tbsp sweetened condensed milk

1 tsp sugar

You will also need:
Single-serve phin

Sit a cup of *cà phê đen nóng* in a hot water bath as it extracts, to keep it warm (see Notes, below). This is a small size coffee that loses its heat very quickly over the long brewing time.

In a bowl, whip the egg yolks, sweetened condensed milk, and sugar at low speed using an electric hand mixer until the mixture is light, creamy, and forms very soft peaks.

Add a teaspoon of the brewed coffee and whisk it through until it becomes slightly frothy.

Pour the egg meringue over the black coffee and serve with a spoon. Stir through before you sip.

Notes:
If you don't have a Vietnamese *phin* filter, you can try a very strong French press or espresso instead. Because consuming raw eggs comes with a risk of salmonella, do so at your own risk. You can sometimes find pasteurized eggs, or, you could whip the egg yolks and sugar in a double boiler and bring them to a temperature of 72°C/160°F (test using a thermometer). This minimizes the risk of salmonella but will result in a different consistency. Make sure to keep whipping the whole time to prevent the eggs from scrambling. Once the eggs reach temperature, immediately place the top of the double boiler into an ice bath to stop further cooking, and mix in the condensed milk.

Cà Phê Cốt Dừa

Coconut Coffee

This modern coffee creation can be found all over Vietnam, but it's especially popular in hot, sticky Hà Nội. It's a cool, sweet, and refreshing drink that helps to combat the humidity: a coconut milk slushie piled on top of an intense cup of black Vietnamese coffee brewed in a *phin* (Vietnamese coffee filter).

2 tbsp sweetened condensed milk

4 tbsp coconut milk or cream from a can (see Notes, below)

1½ cups ice

1 serving of cà phê đen nóng *(hot, black coffee): follow recipe for* cà phê sữa *(milk coffee; see page 196), but omit the condensed milk*

You will also need:
Blender, single-serve phin *(Vietnamese coffee filter), cocktail shaker*

Put the condensed milk, coconut milk or cream, and most of the ice (reserve a few cubes) into a blender. Blend until the ice resembles snow.

Brew the *cà phê đen nóng* in the *phin,* add to a cocktail shaker with the remaining ice cubes, put the lid on the shaker, and immediately shake vigorously until the coffee is frothy. Pour into a serving glass.

Pour the coconut slushie into the coffee, so that it sits in a mound in the middle of the glass.

Serve with a spoon for stirring through while drinking.

Notes:
You'll need undiluted coconut milk or cream for this, like what you find in a can, not a carton. You will also need a high-powered blender with sharp blades to blend the ice properly. If you don't have one, you can purchase shaved ice or crush a regular bag of ice by hand.

Cà Phê Sữa Chua

Yogurt Coffee

Vietnamese cuisine was heavily influenced by the French, and this drink is an excellent example. After the French introduced yogurt (alongside butter, milk, and cheese), the Vietnamese started to experiment with adding some of these dairy products to coffee. It's uncertain when or where adding yogurt to coffee began, but the sweet, thin Vietnamese style of yogurt is now a common addition to black coffee.

1 serving cà phê đen nóng *(hot, black coffee): follow recipe for* cà phê sữa *(milk coffee; see page 196) but omit the condensed milk*

2 tbsp sweetened condensed milk

½ cup plain full-fat yogurt
(see Notes, below)

1 cup crushed ice

You will also need:
Single-serve phin

Brew a cup of *cà phê đen nóng.*

As it extracts, gently mix the condensed milk and yogurt in a serving glass. Pour the crushed ice over the top.

Pour the coffee over the top of the ice, then mix together before serving.

Notes:
You'll need plain yogurt for this recipe. Sweetened is fine, but make sure it's not thick like Greek yogurt. You can also add a pinch of salt before mixing through. Many baristas put their own flair on this coffee—try whizzing the coffee and a couple of ice cubes in a blender to make a coffee slushie before pouring over the yogurt, or swap the *cà phê đen nóng* for a whipped coffee, like the *dalgona* coffee (see page 222).

A Confluence of Flavor in Singapore

Early 1900s, Singapore: Hainanese immigrants, after cooking for British colonial households, began turning vacant shophouses into coffeehouses called *kopitiams*.

The *kopitiams* of Singapore preserve a specialized local coffee culture through adherence to tradition. The word *kopi* means coffee in Malay, while 店 *tiam/diàn* means shop in Hokkien. *Kopitiams* are also found in Malaysia, southern Thailand, Brunei, and Indonesia, with each region having its own unique *kopitiam* culture.

These coffeehouses are usually open-air, relying on ceiling fans to keep the Southeast Asian nation's humidity at bay. A lively community of older folks chat, play games, read the newspaper, and watch the world go by. *Kopitiams* are packed from sunrise with old and young alike, all slurping down the local *kopi* and watching the tropical island city-state wake up.

Local roasters are trained to first coat the coffee beans in molten sugar, a modified form of the European *torrefacto* method. Typically, maize will also be added to the blend. Finally, the roasters add margarine to make sure the sugar-coated beans don't stick together as they cool. This method of roasting enhances the flavor of the *robusta* coffee beans, the species most widely grown in Southeast Asia. Some in the coffee trade claim that the *kopi* roast came about to mask defects in the coffee and to increase the weight of the beans for improved revenue per pound. Whether that is true or not, its unique flavor has become an integral part of local coffee culture.

This style of coffee is known formally as *Nanyang kopi,* and the name attests to the diverse mix of influences that have inspired the local coffee culture. *Nanyang* translates from Chinese as Southern Ocean, a term used by the Chinese to refer to the warmer lands of Southeast Asia.

Singapore's history of immigration and colonization has resulted in a diverse and varied culinary culture. Singaporeans are of predominantly Chinese, Malay, and Indian ethnic origins. There are smatterings of Dutch and British influence from the region's colonial history too, perhaps most visibly in the food scene.

Around the time of British colonization (1819), significant populations emigrated from southern China to Singapore and Malaysia. The wealthier immigrants took over industries such as the textile and spice trades, while the less well-off took on manual labor jobs. The Hainanese were relatively late to immigrate, arriving after the Teochews, Fuzhounese, Fujianese, and others. By the time they came to Singapore, there were few options left for plying a trade, so the Hainanese used the skills they had developed as service workers for colonial households to open coffee shops for the local population. To this day, *kopitiams* are often called *Hainanese kopitiams,* giving credit to the Hainanese for their deep affiliation with the trade. The Hainanese took a staple drink of a nation and elevated it to its current status.

Before the 1980s, *kopi* was usually served in little porcelain or earthenware cups, sporting patterns of flowers in green or blue ink. The saucer was used to serve typical *kopitiam* foods: a very soft-boiled egg, shell on, for customers to crack open and top with →

UCKY
NATOWN

→ pepper and dark soy sauce; or *kaya* toast (*kaya* is a sweet coconut spread), thought to be derived from the toast-loving British colonial households in which many Hainanese cooks worked. While these cups have their origins in China, they are now items of nostalgia for many Singaporeans.

Into these cups, a unique recipe of condensed milk, evaporated milk, coffee, and sugar is blended. The talents of the *kopi* uncle or auntie (or, in earlier days, the *kopi kia* or coffee kid)—as these purveyors of the lifeblood of the nation are affectionately called—are on display. They advertise their skill with great flair amid billows of steam and the wafting fragrance of coffee and caramelized sugar. Every Singaporean has their favorite *kopitiam*—ask anyone who makes the best *kopi* and you'll receive a dozen different adamant recommendations.

There are more than 132 formal combinations, depending on how sweet you like it, and your preferred serving temperature, all the way down to what sort of milk you like.

To brew the dark and intense local *kopi*, the coffee powder is mixed with hot water, then the jet-black liquid is poured in cascades between large steel pitchers. This process, in addition to extracting the coffee evenly, melts the blackened sugar that coats the coffee beans. After a number of pours—the ideal number differs depending on whom you ask—*kopi* is served into either a glass-handled mug or the little patterned ceramic cup, the grounds filtered out through a long cloth filter known locally as a *kopi* sock.

When it comes to ordering, Singapore's diversity really shines through. There are more than 132 formal combinations, depending on how sweet you like it, and your preferred serving temperature, all the way down to what sort of milk you like. There is no real standardized recipe for *kopi* because every brewer has a slightly different ratio, method, or recipe based on their experience, taste, and the *kopi* brand they use.

This style of coffee is known formally as *Nanyang kopi*, and the name attests to the diverse mix of influences that have inspired the local coffee culture. *Nanyang* translates from Chinese as Southern Ocean.

The drink can be easily customized to your preference with the addition of Hokkien or Malay terms. The standard *kopi* is milky and very sweet, mixed with around two tablespoons of condensed milk, while *kopi-O* (black coffee) will come with around two tablespoons of added sugar. Ask for a *kopi C* and the condensed milk is replaced with evaporated milk. The Hokkien term *siew dai* means reduced sweetness, from two tablespoons of sugar to one. *Ga dai* increases the added sugar to three tablespoons, while the Malay word for zero, *kosong*, lets the *kopi* uncle or auntie know you don't want any sugar added at all. Looking for an iced coffee instead? Just add *peng* to any *kopi* order.

(Opposite) The city of Singapore rises above the streets of its Chinatown district. At some of the smaller, family-run coffee stalls and shops, it is not unusual for your coffee to come in a plastic bag with a straw.

Kopi

Coffee

A standard *kopi* is brewed with specially roasted beans that are coated with sugar and margarine. The dark coffee is mixed with creamy condensed milk, making it intensely sweet. Many Singaporeans also drink their *kopi* black (*Kopi-O*), replacing the condensed milk with two tablespoons of sugar.

20 g (4 level tbsp) Nanyang-style coffee
Grind size: fine to medium

200 ml (7 fl oz) hot water
(95°C–98°C/203°F–208°F)

2 tbsp condensed milk

You will also need:
Cloth coffee-sock filter (see Notes, below), *two (preferably metal) pitchers*

Warm your serving cup by filling it with hot water.

Rinse the cloth coffee-sock filter and place it over the rim of one of the metal pitchers. Measure the coffee into the other pitcher and pour the hot water over it when it is at the correct temperature (test using a thermometer). Leave for 30 seconds (the coffee, if fresh, should foam).

If using a fine grind, stir for 30 seconds to 1 minute. For a medium grind, stir and leave to infuse for 3–4 minutes, then give it another quick stir before pouring.

Pour the coffee from the pitcher, through the coffee-sock filter, into the other pitcher.

Tip out the hot water from the serving cup and add the 2 tbsp condensed milk, or to taste. Pour the filtered *kopi* base brew over the top. You should be left with just over ⅔ cup (150 ml/5 fl oz) *kopi* base.

When using *Nanyang kopi*, or coffee beans that have been roasted in sugar, it is usually diluted roughly 2:1 *kopi* to water, or water and milk. If you are using regular-roast coffee, you might not need to dilute as much.

Stir it all together to blend and serve.

Notes:
The beauty of *kopi* is that it is easily customized to your preference: reduce the sugar, add evaporated rather than condensed milk, or dilute with more hot water. The cloth coffee-sock filter is easily found online, or in many Asian grocery stores. *Nanyang kopi* roast is integral for the flavor of this brew, but if you can't find this type of roast, see if you can track down *torrefacto* coffee instead.

Kopi Gu You

SERVES 1

Butter Coffee

While the rest of the world has only recently started whizzing grass-fed butter and coconut oil into their morning brews, Singaporeans have been adding a lump of butter to their coffee since the early 1900s.

1 cup kopi *(see method, page 208)*

½ tbsp butter (unsalted is best)

Brew a standard cup of *kopi,* but don't stir the condensed milk through yet.

Float the butter on top. Unsalted butter is commonly used at *kopitiams,* but you can use salted butter if you prefer.

When the butter has melted, stir and mix just before taking your first sip.

Notes:

You could also brew any other *kopi* variant and add butter to it. If you'd prefer an unsweetened version, try it with *kopi-O-kosong:* black coffee with no sugar.

From Gunboat Diplomacy to Instant Success in Korea

Mid-1900s, Seoul: coffee and teahouses called *dabangs* (다방) proliferated as cultural meeting places after decades of colonial occupation, war, and unrest. Their growth was aided by U.S. military rations of instant coffee, which helped the dabangs to serve coffee without any specialized equipment.

Korea's relationship with coffee is, as is often the case, inextricably linked with politics. Coffee's journey around the world from its origin in Africa was often aided by colonial consumption, cultivation, and commerce.

Before the late 1800s, Korea's foreign associations were largely limited to China and Japan. Coffee was not widely consumed in China nor Japan at this time, so it is unlikely that coffee was introduced to Korea before the late 1800s—although there are no clear records of the origin or timing of the first coffee to arrive on Korea's shores.

In 1876, during the Joseon Dynasty (Korea's last dynasty), Emperor Gojong signed the Japan-Korea Treaty. Up until then, foreign trade had been very limited because the Korean government was wary of foreign ships. The Japanese, however, employed classic gunboat diplomacy to prevail upon the Emperor to sign the treaty. The Japanese won favorable terms, including the opening up of three Korean ports to trade. Later, in 1910, Japan annexed Korea, beginning 35 years of colonial rule.

Coffee, which had first arrived in Japan on Dutch ships in the 1700s and 1800s, was already a feature of Japanese society by the time the colonial era began. The colonial emphasis on assimilation policies and the desire to extend the influence of Japanese culture certainly helped to increase coffee consumption in Korea.

The popular story is that Emperor Gojong was the first person to try coffee in Korea, when a Russian ambassador's sister served him a cup in 1896. This story is perhaps more fanciful than accurate because there are numerous earlier records. Perhaps the earliest is by the American Percival Lowell, who was invited to visit Korea after escorting diplomats on the first Korean Special Mission to the United States. In his subsequent book, *Chosön, the Land of the Morning Calm,* Lowell writes that, "In January 1884, a governor of the province invited me to the House of the Sleeping Waves, and we had after-dinner coffee, the latest trend in Joseon."

Coffee is frequently mentioned in historical texts over the following years. While initially drunk by royalty and the upper class, coffee's popularity spread quickly. According to Park Young-soon in his book, *Coffee Humanities* (커피인문학), the first written record of a coffeehouse opening was in 1899 in Seoul, and Park writes that coffee was sold by street vendors in the early 1900s. Park also notes that rumors of black coffee being an effective roundworm medicine helped boost its popularity.

In subsequent decades, Korean consumer products were heavily influenced by Japanese and Western cultures. While it is easy to surmise that the coffee-drinking trend grew substantially during the colonial →

Oriole
Green

→ era, there is little written record of coffee culture during Japanese colonial rule.

By the early to mid-twentieth century, coffee and teahouses called *dabangs* (다방) were ubiquitous. Much like the coffeehouses of Europe, these were important gathering places for people engaged in political dissent, as well as writers, poets, and the general public.

> The popular story is that Emperor Gojong was the first person to try coffee in Korea, when a Russian ambassador's sister served him a cup in 1896.

At the end of the Second World War, the U. S. military swept in with large rations of instant coffee, some of which found their way into South Korean society. In his book, Park suggests that the introduction of instant coffee helped the proliferation of the *dabangs* because instant coffee required no special brewing equipment.

> By the early to mid-twentieth century, coffee and teahouses called *dabangs* were ubiquitous. Much like the coffeehouses of Europe, these were important gathering places for people engaged in political dissent.

The American food giant General Foods supplied its brand Maxwell House instant coffee to the U. S. Armed Forces. The name Maxwell House became so connected with coffee in Korea that in the 1970s Maxwell House was licensed for domestic production. The production of instant coffee in Korea led to an explosion in coffee consumption, helping to move coffee from the *dabangs* into the home.

Today, the *dabangs* from 100 years ago take a back seat to specialty cafés selling drip-brewed coffee. Koreans tend to associate the term *dabang* coffee with instant coffee.

For a couple of decades now, innovative specialty roasters and coffee professionals have been pushing the industry forward. Korea has built itself a reputation as a hub for specialty coffee, and Seoul annually hosts Asia's largest coffee festival. There are even specialty coffee shops near the DMZ, the demilitarized zone on the border with North Korea.

Some Korean cafés, particularly in Seoul, take a novel approach to finishing touches—cute faces floating on the surface of a drink (page 213), or stenciled with cocoa (following pages), and marshmallow creatures rising from the froth.

COFFEE
COFFEE
COFFEE
COFFEE
COFFEE

ZAPANGI
TIN AND BOTTLE

달고나 커피 Dalgona keopi

SERVES 1

Dalgona Coffee

This coffee is named for its similarity in flavor and appearance to honeycomb candy, called *dalgona* in Korean. Although it has been recently popularized by Koreans, it most likely originated elsewhere. A number of countries have been making this coffee for years, including India and Pakistan, where it is called *phitti hui, phenti hui,* or *pheta* coffee.

2 tbsp instant coffee

2 tbsp granulated sugar

2 tbsp hot water

1 cup iced or hot milk

You will also need:

Hand blender with whisk attachment or mixer (optional)

Put the instant coffee, sugar, and water in a mixing bowl and whip until the mixture is thick, pale, and creamy. It will take at least 2–3 minutes. If you are whipping by hand, it could take 8–10 minutes or more.

Pour the milk into a glass, and spoon the whipped coffee mixture over the top.

Stir through before drinking.

Notes:

You have to use instant coffee and sugar for this recipe; it won't work with regular brewed coffee. The dehydration process and addition of emulsifiers in instant coffee results in a creamier, foamier beverage once blended. Sugar increases the viscosity, holding the foaminess for longer. You can also make this with hot, steamed milk, or chilled milk for an iced coffee.

모닝 커피 Morning keopi

SERVES 1

Morning Coffee

In Korea's 다방 *dabangs* (coffeehouses) an egg yolk was often added to a cup of black coffee: it was thought the egg yolk would make the coffee less harsh on an empty stomach. This drink—now out of fashion but common in the mid-twentieth century—was known as morning *keopi*, as it was very popular as a breakfast and beverage in one.

1 cup black coffee

1 egg

2–3 drops toasted sesame oil

Brew a cup of black coffee using your preferred method. In Korea, instant coffee is favored, but you could use a cup of French press or any method that makes a regular-sized black filter coffee.

Crack the egg and separate the white and yolk. Lift the yolk with a spoon and sprinkle the sesame oil on top. Carefully place the yolk into the black coffee and stir through.

Notes:

Consuming raw eggs comes with a risk of salmonella. Use pasteurized eggs, if available, or make this drink at your own risk. As with many traditional recipes, some coffee shops and home brewers often add their own ingredients. Many morning coffee recipes call for the addition of a small pinch of salt on top of the egg yolk before stirring it into the coffee, and to top the brew with a scattering of pine nuts or chopped walnuts.

Coffee, Cake, and Invention

1700s, Vienna, Austria: The Viennese coffee house was consolidating its place in society, spawning coffee recipes, traditions, baked goods, and design styles that remain internationally renowned today.

When and where the first coffeehouse in Europe opened is a topic of keen debate. While some claim the credit for Serbia or Hungary in the 1500s, others insist that it was in Vienna or Venice, citing Ottoman influence through either trade or war. Vienna, a city now known worldwide for its opulent traditional cafés and coffee shops, has a deep-rooted coffee history that has spawned distinctive recipes and influential traditions. Officially recognized by UNESCO as having "Intangible Cultural Heritage," Viennese Coffee House Culture is a point of cultural pride for Austrians and a key draw for visitors.

The origin story of the first *Wiener kaffeehaus* (Viennese coffeehouse) is, like many origin stories relating to coffee, subject to much mythologization. The popular story goes that a Polish diplomat by the name of Jerzy Franciszek Kulczycki opened Vienna's first coffeehouse after being given a number of bags of strange-looking beans, obtained after the Polish-Habsburg army liberated Vienna from the Turks during the Siege of Vienna in 1683. Kulczycki is also often credited with the introduction of milk into coffee, which, along with the addition of sugar, popularized the bitter brew for the masses. While this story is still prevalent in popular culture—and many Viennese coffeehouses still pay homage to Kulczycki—more recent research attributes the first Viennese coffeehouse to the Armenian or Greek diplomat/spy Deodato, who was entrusted with brewing coffee for the Habsburg court in Vienna.

Regardless of how it got its start, the Viennese coffeehouse soon became the public's living room, as coffeehouses would do in other cities around the world. The caffeinated fervor of these establishments was the main draw. Packed with intellectuals, writers, businessmen, dissidents, and spies, coffeehouses were meeting places, hothouses of debate, and community gathering places. Men from all walks of life shared in discussion, stories, and knowledge. Particular establishments became known as meeting places for those sharing a specific interest. Coffeehouses were frequented by notable historical figures including Sigmund Freud, Gustav Klimt, Arthur Schnitzler, Leon Trotzky.

Austrian columnist Alfred Polgar (1926, as cited in Segel, 1995) said that coffeehouse patrons were "people who want to be alone but need companionship for it." This maxim supports the concept of the coffeehouse as "third place:" a term coined by American urban sociologist Ray Oldenburg.

The "third place" is a social environment, separate from the two usual social environments of home ("first place") and the workplace ("second place"). Oldenburg argues that third places are important for civil society, democracy, civic engagement, and for building a sense of place—all of which became integral parts of coffeehouse culture. The coffeehouse was also a place for solitary enjoyment: it was (and still is) a common phenomenon for people to spend hours alone, reading newspapers, and journals while sipping coffee.

In addition to the social aspects, Viennese coffeehouses became known for their style, palatial design, upholstered decor, creative coffee drinks, rituals, and pastries. The best bakers invented and served cakes →

CAFE
SCHWARZENBERG

→ and pastries that gained Vienna an international reputation. Countless coffee recipes evolved, inspired by local tastes and coffee traditions from abroad.

Today, you can find dozens of variations on coffee recipes in the Viennese coffeehouse. The *kleiner/großer* schwarzer (smaller/larger black) are similar to the espressos you would find elsewhere, while the *kleiner/großer brauner* (smaller/larger brown) are served with milk or cream on the side to add as you prefer. The *einspänner* is a popular order, the name referring to either a one-horse carriage or an espresso topped with whipped cream. The story goes that the drink was invented to be drunk with one hand while driving the carriage—the cream preventing spillage and keeping it warm.

Initially the coffeehouses were reserved for men. In response, women devised the *kaffeekränzchen* (coffee circle), a private gathering at home over coffee and cake.

The *kapuziner,* the forerunner of the modern cappuccino, is a varied mixture of coffee (sometimes with sugar) that is topped with cream, and is said to have gained its name by having a similar brown colour to the robes of the Capuchin friars in Vienna and elsewhere. The *mélange* is a drink that is more similar to the modern-day cappuccino, except that there is usually hot water added to the espresso and the milk is foamed into even more copious froth.

In the Viennese coffeehouses, many types of liquor or alcohol were mixed with coffee. The *biedermeier* is a *kleiner/großer brauner* mixed with apricot liqueur and topped with whipped cream; the *Maria Theresia* (named after the Holy Roman Empress) is a black coffee mixed with orange liqueur and topped with whipped cream.

In Germany, coffee-drinking spread through the country much as it did in the rest of Europe—first through the ruling classes in the 1600s and 1700s, and then to other parts of German society. As was the case elsewhere, initially the coffeehouses were reserved for men. In response, women devised the *kaffeekränzchen* (coffee circle), a private gathering at home over coffee and cake. Their inception was revolutionary, as it afforded women the opportunity for social gathering outside the realms of productive work.

However, during the late-eighteenth century, Germany underwent a period of social conflict that resulted in the enactment of anti-coffee legislation. Health, social, and economic reasons were cited: those who opposed coffee consumption were concerned that workers were becoming too accustomed to the "leisure time" a coffee break afforded, and, as detailed by Liberles (2012) many felt that "class lines were threatened by a provocative sense of change that had begun with the expanded consumption of [coffee]."

Consequently, new legislation decreed that the poor were not allowed to drink coffee, although the wealthy were free to do so. Frederick the Great is perhaps the leader most connected to the anti-coffee legislation (it is said he was more partial to tobacco than coffee). He instituted heavy taxes on coffee and other "luxury goods," which simply resulted in a thriving black-market trade. He employed soldiers to wander the streets sniffing out illegally roasting coffee. These men became known as *kaffeeriechers* (coffee sniffers), and they fined anyone found roasting coffee without the required permits.

After Frederick's death, much of the legislation was lifted, and Germany resumed its obsession with coffee in full force. As the obsession grew, Germans came up with a number of world-changing inventions and discoveries. In the early 1900s, two key inventions were to change coffee-brewing and consumption forever.

The first was the discovery of decaffeination. A team led by the German merchant Ludwig Roselius applied for a patent in 1906 for a process that steamed the coffee bean in seawater, extracting the caffeine without the use of solvents. Originally, the team used benzene, and, while other solvents are used today, the method is quite similar to the initial invention.

The pour-over method using a paper filter was born when Melitta Bentz punched holes through the base of a brass pot and placed a piece of blotting paper from her son's school notebook over it.

Around the same time, Melitta Bentz, a housewife from Dresden, Germany, revolutionized the art of coffee brewing. The pour-over method using a paper filter was born when she punched holes through the base of a brass pot and placed a piece of blotting paper from her son's school notebook over it. This controlled-filtration method produced a very different cup profile from that of the brewing methods that preceded it (the most similar method would have been filtering the coffee through a rough cloth). Her invention, the Melitta coffee filter, for which she was awarded a patent in 1908, remains the precursor to many specialty brew methods today.

Meanwhile, in the early 1900s in Switzerland, a brand that was to change how the world consumed coffee at home was gathering strength. New Zealand, Japanese, British, and French inventors and chemists have been credited with inventing instant coffee, depending on the source, however it was Swiss food giant, Nestlé (leaders in the condensed milk and chocolate markets) who brought it to the world. Max Morgenthaler, a chemist working for Nestlé during the global coffee crisis of the 1920s and '30s, was set to work on a project focused on flavor and convenience.

The bank, which owned an excess of beans in Brazil, held immense volumes of coffee after the price crash (see page 147). Nestlé was tasked to help in making use of the surplus. Morgenthaler set about creating soluble coffee that preserved the taste and aroma of a fresh cup. The initial target market was Swiss single men, who could then make a delicious cup easily without needing to actually brew it. Launched in 1938, Nescafé was a hit—and given Nestlé's existing international reach, it was not long before it was on shelves worldwide.

The war that broke out soon after spurred sales, as instant coffee ended up being an excellent product for soldiers' military rations. It was easy to brew when little else was available, requiring no equipment beyond that required to heat water. The entire production of the Nescafé U. S. plant—about a million cases a year—was reserved for military use during the Second World War.

In a coffeehouse, one can spend the entire day. In the afternoon, the combination of coffee and pastries enjoys great popularity.

SACHER
ORIGINAL SACHER-TORTE
Hotel Sacher
WIEN

Konditorei
PATISSERIE
CAFE CENTRAL
RESTAURANT

Kaisermelange

Coffee with Egg Yolk and Honey

An Austrian specialty once popular in Vienna, this coffee drink is not commonly found on menus these days. An egg yolk and honey are whipped together to create a creamy sweet topping, and Cognac is often added to spike the mix. This drink is not to be confused with the *mélange* (see page 229), another Austrian coffee drink similar to a cappuccino.

1 egg yolk

1 tsp honey

1 cup strong black coffee

30 ml (1 fl oz) Cognac (optional)

Put the egg yolk and honey into your serving cup, and, using a fork, spoon, or a small whisk, mix together until frothy.

Brew your cup of hot coffee, then pour slowly into the egg and honey mixture while mixing well.

Add 30 ml (1 fl oz) of Cognac at the end before serving, if using, to serve.

Notes:

Consuming raw eggs comes with a risk of salmonella. Use pasteurized eggs, if available, or make this drink at your own risk. Alternatively, you could whip the egg yolks and honey in the top of a double boiler and bring them up to a temperature of 72 °C/160°F (test using a thermometer). This process minimizes the risk of salmonella, but will result in a different consistency. Make sure to keep whipping the whole time to prevent the eggs from scrambling. Once the mixture reaches temperature, immediately place the top of the double boiler into an ice bath to stop further cooking, then mix in the coffee, adding the Cognac, if using.

Kafi Luz

SERVES 1

Coffee with Brandy

Also known as *kafi/kaffee fertig*, or *kaffe Träsch*, this is a popular hot coffee drink mixed with Träsch (also called Bätzi), a Swiss fruit brandy usually made from apples and pears. It should be very pale and thin. You should be able to read a newspaper through it.

120 ml (4 fl oz) weak black coffee

2–3 cubes of sugar, to taste

45 ml (1½ fl oz) of pear and / or apple brandy

Brew your coffee weakly. It should be light in color, almost like tea. To do this, simply reduce the ratio of coffee to water you would usually use.

Put your preferred amount of sugar in a serving glass and pour the hot coffee over the top. Add the brandy.

Notes:

In the traditional recipe, the sugar is put into a serving glass and just enough coffee is added so that you can no longer see the sugar. Brandy is then added until the mixture is clear enough to see the sugar again. There are a number of Swiss variations that use plum, pear, or apple brandy with coffee. You could also try the *schümli-pflümli*, made with equal parts coffee and Zwetschgen plum schnapps (made from a damson-like plum popular in Central Europe), and topped with whipped cream.

Franziskaner

Coffee with Cream

The *franziskaner*, like the *kapuziner*, gained its name from the color created after blending coffee and milk/cream: the same color as the robes of Franciscan friars (*Franziskaner*) or Capuchin friars (*Kapuziner*). The *kapuziner* is coffee (sometimes topped with a little water) and whipped cream, while the *franziskaner* often uses a little less coffee and includes milk.

60 ml (2 fl oz) whipping cream

30 ml (1 fl oz) espresso (see page 34)

60 ml (2 fl oz) steamed or hot milk

cocoa powder, for dusting

Whip the cream in a bowl until it forms stiff peaks when the whisk is removed.

Brew your espresso into a serving cup. Steam the milk if you have a steamer, or heat the milk in a pan over medium heat. Add the hot milk to the espresso.

Spoon over the with whipped cream and dust with cocoa powder to serve.

Notes:

Some recipes call for the espresso to be watered down a little. Try adding 30 ml (1 fl oz) water to your espresso before the milk to change the taste.

Eiskaffee

Coffee with Ice Cream

This coffee-and-ice cream delight was most likely invented in Germany, although it often goes by the name *Wiener Eiskaffee* and is a popular drink in Switzerland, Austria, and at Viennese coffeehouses, as well as throughout Germany. Originally, it consisted of a cup of black coffee poured over scoops of ice cream, although modern versions are often made with espresso or coffee with milk. No matter what, the drink must include coffee, ice cream, and whipped cream and is usually topped with cocoa powder or sprinkles.

60 ml (2 fl oz) cup whipping cream

1 cup strong black coffee or 60 ml (2 fl oz) espresso (see page 34)

2 scoops vanilla ice cream

cocoa powder or chocolate flakes for dusting

Whip the cream in a bowl until it forms stiff peaks when the whisk is removed.

Brew your cup of coffee or espresso, then chill in the fridge.

Place scoops of ice cream in a tall serving glass, then pour the chilled coffee over. Spoon over with the whipped cream and dust with cocoa powder or chocolate flakes and serve.

Notes:

For variations, you can just pour the hot coffee over the ice cream to melt it a little so it's easier to mix through your coffee. This will be similar to the Italian *affogato*, in which the sweet ice cream melts into black coffee. You could also pour a little milk into chilled black coffee then pour it over ice cream. You can also experiment with different ice cream flavors.

Pharisäer

Coffee with Rum

The origin myth of this rum-and-coffee drink goes that the parishioners of a North Frisian Island spiked the coffee to hide their alcohol consumption from their non-alcohol-loving pastor, topping the drink with whipped cream so the scent of the rum wouldn't waft out of the cup. It is said that the pastor was served the same coffee without alcohol, but once he got a whiff of the rum in other cups shouted, "Ihr Pharisäer!," a reference to the accusation of hypocrisy towards the Pharisees in the Bible.

60 ml (2 fl oz) whipping cream

1 cup strong black coffee

45 ml (1½ fl oz) dark rum

Whip the cream in a bowl until it forms stiff peaks when the whisk is removed.

Brew your cup of hot coffee, then pour it into a serving glass. Add the rum then spoon over the whipped cream. Traditionally, this is not stirred through, but sipped through the cream.

Notes:

The *Pharisäer kaffee* traditionally uses rum, but you could make a regional variation such as the *Rüdesheimer Kaffee*. Simply switch the rum to brandy and flambé a sugar cube in the alcohol before adding the coffee and whipped cream.

CAFE

Subsistence and Resistance in The Nordics

Eighteenth century, Sápmi, northern Europe: Indigenous Sámi people topped coffee with reindeer milk cheese (*gáffevuosta*), dried reindeer meat, or *maŋŋebuoidi*, the fat from reindeer intestine.

The Nordic countries, or Nordics, are a geographic and cultural region encompassing a significant area of northern Europe. Norway, Sweden, Iceland, Finland, Denmark, and the Faroe Islands are all Nordic countries, and their residents consume a remarkable amount of coffee—particularly the indigenous Sámi people, who inhabit Sápmi in the far north of the region. William H. Ukers noted in his book *All About Coffee,* published in 1922, that Sweden had the highest per-capita coffee consumption in the world. The trend has continued: Nordic countries regularly place among the top five for the volume of coffee consumed per capita.

Coffee was imported into Sweden sometime around the late 1600s, and into other Nordic countries soon after, although the beverage had a rocky start. Sweden alternated between banning and heavily taxing coffee throughout the eighteenth and nineteenth centuries, although the populace never complied with the prohibitions. Smuggling was rife, and coffee quickly became a drink for the common man—not only the bourgeoisie.

The famous Swedish botanist Carolus Linnaeus (also known as Carl von Linné), regarded as the father of modern taxonomy, first classified the genus *Coffea* in 1737. Linnaeus derided coffee for causing ill health and also held the nationalist opinion (common in Europe at that time) that coffee, as a foreign product, was damaging to Sweden's economy and culture.

Linnaeus and a number of other doctors and naturalists spent a good deal of time looking for local coffee substitutes. Hanna Hodacs notes in *Coffee and Coffee Surrogates in Sweden* that beech nuts, burnt bread, fava beans, acorns, sunflower seeds, oats, juniper berries, maize, rye, chicory, chestnuts, peanuts, lupine seeds, carrots, potatoes, and black or red currant seeds were suggested in various historical records as coffee substitutes. Often, some of these substances were blended with actual coffee to stretch the supply and to tailor the drink to specific or regional tastes.

Today, the tradition of *fika* is a common part of many Swedes' daily rituals. The word, said to be an inversion of the two syllables of the Swedish word for coffee (*kaffe*), is both a verb and a noun. *Fika* refers to both making time to take a break, slow down, reset, or meet with friends, as well as the cup of coffee and *kaffebröd* (coffee bread or baked good) eaten at the time.

Anna Brones and Johanna Kindvall note in their book *Fika: The Art of the Swedish Coffee Break* that *fika*, particularly for the older generations, is about so much more than grabbing a coffee. "*Ska vi fika?* (Should we *fika?*) means 'Let's take a break, spend some time together, slow down.'" Coffee is used as an ingredient in many *fika* snacks, too, such as the ubiquitous *chokladbollar* (chocolate balls).

In Norway and Sweden, especially in rural areas, adding moonshine to coffee has been popular since the 1800s. This strong drink goes by many names: *kaffedoktor* (coffee doctor), *kaffegök*, *karsk*, or *uddevallare*, depending on the region. The recipe changes too, →

EVA HARR

S:T
PAUL
BAGERI

→ depending on where you drink it—some are mixed with brandy (or cognac). But the folkloric recipe remains consistent: drop a coin into the bottom of a cup, and then pour coffee in until you can't see it any longer. Then, pour liquor in until you can see the coin again.

In Norway and Sweden, especially in rural areas, adding moonshine to coffee has been popular since the 1800s. This strong drink goes by many names: *kaffedoktor* (coffee doctor), *kaffegök*, *karsk*, or *uddevallare*, depending on the region.

The Danes also love their *kaffepunch* (coffee with schnapps and sugar). In the 1860s, southern Jutland came under German rule. People came together in town halls to hold meetings and sing Danish songs, but the German authorities would not allow alcohol to be served at meetings. Not content with ending these meetings without the traditional kaffepunch, the *sønderjysk kaffebord* (southern Jutland coffee table) tradition began.

The Danes "met for coffee" instead, filling the table with cakes and baked goods, and serving as much *kaffepunch* as they liked. The German authorities had no say in what happened during these informal gatherings, and attendees were free to drink and spout Danish-minded rhetoric as they pleased. As attendees would often each bring a cake, an element of competitiveness was introduced. Today, *sønderjysk kaffebord* is a continuing tradition in which a veritable feast of baked goods and coffee are served.

In Denmark, the *Madam Blå* (Madame Blue) enameled coffee pot is an iconic feature of twentieth-century Danish households. This coffee pot influenced coffee culture in Denmark. It came in a range of sizes, from 1 to 50 cups, and was designed to be brewed in the morning and left on the stove for serving instantly throughout the day. The factory closed down in 1966, but many kitchens and cafés still hold on to their enameled coffee pots as items of nostalgia.

The culture of the indigenous Sámi people who inhabit Sápmi (a region that encompasses a large part of northern Norway, Sweden, Finland, and Russia) is shaped by the extremely cold environment they traditionally inhabited. Many Sámi people were engaged in reindeer herding and relied on their semi-wild herds for much of their food. Anne Wuolab, interviewed for the chapter "Saami Coffee Culture" in the book *Indigenous Efflorescence: Beyond Revitalisation in Sapmi and Ainu Mosir*, says that coffee was originally used as a complement to reindeer broth, although it was not long before coffee became an important part of Sámi cuisine in its own right.

Today, the tradition of *fika* is a common part of many Swedes' daily rituals. *Fika* refers to both making time to take a break, slow down, reset, or meet with friends, as well as the cup of coffee and *kaffebröd* eaten at the time.

To prepare coffee, the Sámi would traditionally beat the coffee beans inside a *gáffeseahkka* (reindeer-leather coffee bag) with a piece of wood. Then, after the grounds were boiled in water over a fire, *vuoššat gáffe* (cooked coffee, usually just called *gáffe*, or *kokkaffe* in Swedish and Norwegian) is served in a handcrafted *guksi* (wooden cup carved from a birch burl). In spring, when fresh reindeer milk was available, it was added to the coffee.

In *Sámi Food: examples of food traditions as a basis for modern Sámi cuisine*, the Sámi Parliament details a coffee tradition that includes *guhkies-buejtie* (South Sámi language), a sort of sausage made from the innermost part of a reindeer's large intestine. This was dried, sliced, and then added to coffee. *Maŋŋebuoidi* (North Sámi language) refers to the rectum of the reindeer, which was filled with so much fat that it was sometimes used like cream in coffee. This is called *båeries-buejtie* in South Sámi, meaning the elders sausage, because it was given to the family elders.

Known as *kaffeost* in Sweden, *leipäjuusto* in Finland, and *gáffevuosta* in Sámi, coffee cheese was traditionally made with reindeer milk but is now also made with cow or goat milk.

While this particular tradition has all but vanished, the tradition of adding cheese to coffee or serving it with dried meat or reindeer tongue has continued. Known as *kaffeost* in Sweden, *leipäjuusto* in Finland, and *gáffevuosta* in Sámi, coffee cheese was traditionally made with reindeer milk but is now also made with cow or goat milk. It has a consistency similar to halloumi and softens a little when placed in hot coffee. Some Sámi people used coffee beans as markers while playing *tablut*, a Sámi variant of the ancient Nordic *hnefatafl* games that are played on a checkerboard.

In Greenland, the Inuit fell under the spell of the intoxicating brew, too. In the nineteenth century, Danish administrators wrote back home that the Inuit of Greenland had become so fiercely addicted to coffee that they were both starving and freezing as a consequence. In exchange for coffee rations, they had traded the sealskins they needed for clothing and to build the kayaks they needed to hunt for food and more fur. In 1896, American geologist George Frederick Wright recorded an Inuit tradition of carrying around a coffee bean in one's pocket to ensure long life.

Outside the region, many people have heard of Swedish egg coffee, in which an egg is added to the coffee grounds to help clarify the brew. Yet, as it turns out, this method is not particularly Swedish. Joy K. Lintelman surmises in her paper *A Hot Heritage: Swedish Americans and Coffee* that Swedish immigrant women would likely have learned to prepare coffee this way when working as domestic servants in America. Over time, the drink became associated with Swedish-Americans, but people in many countries used eggs or eggshells to clarify unfiltered coffee. A similar method of clarification with a protein was employed in the Nordic countries, but more often it was with *klarskinn* (fish skin) which was added until the grounds settled then removed before drinking.

Scandinavian cities boast a vibrant cafe culture with independents and chain outlets on the same streets. Brewing a pot over an open fire is also a long-established hiking tradition (page 255).

COFFEE

COFFE

Vuostagáffe

SERVES 5–6

Cheese Coffee

The indigenous Sámi people of northern Sweden, Finland, and Norway traditionally added slices of reindeer milk cheese (called *gáffevuosta*), dried reindeer meat, or reindeer fat to their coffee. Reindeer milk cheese is still a common addition to a cup of black coffee to make *vuostagáffe* (cheese coffee, called *kaffeost* in Swedish), although the cheese is more often made with goat's or cow's milk these days.

⅛ tsp liquid calcium chloride (omit if using unpasteurized milk)

1.9 liters (2 quarts) full-fat milk (unpasteurized, if possible)

½ tsp salt

¼ tsp liquid rennet or ¼ rennet tablet

¼ cup unchlorinated cold water

1 cup black coffee per serving

You will also need:
Thermometer, large square cheesecloth

If using pasteurized milk, add the calcium chloride to the milk and set aside for 1 hour. Mix the rennet into the ¼ cup of unchlorinated cold water.

Put the milk (or milk and calcium chloride) in a saucepan over a low heat, stir, and heat to 37°C (99°F); test using a thermometer. Remove from the heat.

Stir the warm milk off the heat. Add the salt and rennet while stirring, then continue to stir for 2 minutes using an up, down, and across motion.

Leave the pan off the heat for 30–40 minutes for the milk to coagulate. Do not stir during this time.

When the time is up, insert a knife directly down, carefully, and slightly turn it (about 40 degrees). The curd should break cleanly and the space created should fill with whey. If the cheese has not coagulated yet, wait a little longer then try the test again in a different part of the milk. Once the milk has successfully coagulated, use the knife to cut slits up and down and across, creating large squares of curd.

Return the pan to a very low heat, stirring gently until the mixture comes back up to 37°C (99°F) (test using a thermometer). Remove from the heat.

Gently ladle the curds into a large square of wet cheesecloth lining a large sieve or strainer, allowing the whey to seep out. Leave to stand for at least 30 minutes. Fold the sides of the cheesecloth over the top of the cheese, and press the curds together. Leave the cheesecloth folded over the cheese.

Place a heavy object directly on top of the cheese to press out more whey. You could use a small chopping board with a weight on top, a small saucepan filled with water, or a dutch oven. Anything that can sit inside the strainer comfortably, and press down on the cheese.

After 15 minutes, check if the curds have stuck together enough to stay in a fairly solid mass when you lift one side. If not, leave to press for longer.

Heat the oven to 230°C (450°F). Transfer the curds to a greased baking dish no larger than the size of the cheese disk. Bake in the hot oven until brown spots appear on the surface. This will take at least 30–40 minutes. Remove and leave to cool.

When the cheese is cooled, you should be able to slice it into chunks. Add a few to each cup of strong black coffee—it should puff up a little and soften.

Notes:

Traditionally, the cheese was pressed for a long period and then dried, which made the cheese firm enough that it did not dissolve in the hot coffee. We use the method of baking to speed up the drying process. You can also try mixing some cream with your milk (keeping the amount of liquid the same) to make a more flavorsome cheese. Rennet and calcium chloride are commonly used cheese-making ingredients and are readily available online. While both are easiest to use in liquid form, you can also get calcium chloride crystals or rennet in a paste, powder, or tablet. Any of these can be substituted; just make sure rennet tablets are ground down and dissolved in ¼ cup cold water before adding to the milk.

Kalaallit Kaffiat

Greenlandic Coffee

This warming blend of alcohol and coffee is the perfect antidote to a cold Arctic winter. It's said to be representative of all parts of Greenland: whisky for the rough side, coffee liqueur for the feminine, delicate side, and orange brandy liqueur set alight and poured in a sparkling stream onto the snowy whipped cream, representing the northern lights.

1½ tbsp whisky

1½ tbsp coffee liqueur (such as Kahlúa)

1 cup hot black coffee

3 tbsp whipped cream

1 tsp orange brandy liqueur (such as Grand Marnier)

Pour the whisky and coffee liqueur into a serving cup; then pour the coffee over the top. Stir through.

Top with the whipped cream, then measure out the orange brandy liqueur into a flame-proof spoon. Carefully set it alight (you might not be able to see the flame), and let it burn for 5 seconds before pouring it over the top of the whipped cream carefully.

Notes:

Often served alongside *kalaallit kaagiat* (Greenlandic tea cake with raisins) at a *kaffemik* (literally via coffee), which is an all-day open-house party at which friends and family drop in and out as they please. You can make this in a larger batch and change the ratio of alcohol to coffee too.

Arabica
the common name for *Coffea arabica*, of which there are many varieties and cultivars. *Arabica* is the dominant coffee species in commercial production, and is often regarded as the epitome of quality. *Arabica* comprises more than 70 percent of the world's coffee production and makes up the vast majority of coffee sold as specialty coffee.

Cascara/qishr
means skin or husk and refers to the dried skins of coffee cherries, which can be brewed to make tea or soda.

Coffee rust
a disease caused by a fungus (*Hemileia vastatrix*) that infects coffee trees. The disease has plagued farmers worldwide for more than a century, threatening coffee supply.

Commodity coffee
is traded on the commodities market in the same way as cotton, timber, copper, and many other products. The high volumes in which coffee of this standard is traded require products from many different farms, so commodity coffee tends to be judged on its ability to meet minimum standards rather than on its unique characteristics.

Crema
the light layer of foam that sits atop espresso. *Crema* is the result of several factors combined with pressure extraction. When particular types of coffee are brewed with hot water forced through the coffee grounds at pressure (such as in an espresso machine), carbon dioxide is released, which combines with the water to create foam.

Cupping
the professional method for evaluating coffee beans. Tasters rank various qualities in the brewed coffee (such as body, fragrance/aroma, balance, sweetness, acidity, and aftertaste) out of 10, combining for a total score out of 100 on the sensory scale.

Direct trade
a contentious, often misused term used to describe the process of buying coffee beans straight from farmers, rather than through a traditional trading network. As the term is unregulated and often used incorrectly, many roasters instead choose to make their own direct trade models public, which often include ethical, moral, sustainable, social, environmental, and fair price philosophies.

Flavor profile
describes a coffee's overall taste, taking into account inherent characteristics and processing decisions. The coffee species and variety determine one element of the flavor; others come about through fermentation and drying; roasting processes and the way in which the beans are brewed also contribute. Flavor profiles may be described using terms such as fruity, sweet, clean, acidic, toasty, caramel, or nutty.

Green coffee
coffee beans that have been dried and are ready for export to roasters. Coffee beans are often a light yellow green before they have been roasted.

Liberica
the common name for *Coffea liberica*, a type of coffee with commercial relevance primarily in Southeast Asia. It has the lowest caffeine content of the commercially relevant coffee species.

Peaberry

occurs when only one seed develops in the coffee cherry instead of the usual two. Some people incorrectly believe that the peaberry is a variety of coffee grown in Tanzania, is a mutation, or that Tanzania produces more peaberry coffee than other places. Peaberries can occur anywhere and make up only 5–10 percent of any given harvest.

Roast, light/medium/dark

are terms used to describe the degree to which coffee beans are roasted. Chemical reactions that take place when heat is applied cause the beans to turn from green to brown and continue to darken the longer they are roasted. The color can help a coffee drinker to select beans to suit their tastes.

Roastery

a relatively new term that was introduced into the coffee industry lexicon primarily to describe the location in which coffee beans are roasted. It may have come about to reduce confusion because the term coffee roaster can refer to many different things: the person who roasts the coffee, a company focused on coffee roasting, or the actual machine itself.

Robusta

Coffea robusta is a variety of *Coffea canephora*, although the commercial significance of this single variety has led to *robusta* becoming widely used as the common name for the species. It is higher in caffeine content and easier to grow than *arabica*.

SCA

the Specialty Coffee Association, a nonprofit organization with main offices in the United States and the United Kingdom, bringing together farmers, baristas, and roasters. The organization acts to unify the industry by holding events, raising standards, and providing resources for all supply chain stages.

Single-origin

coffee beans sourced from a single geographical location, either from one farm or a group of farms.

Specialty coffee

very high-quality coffees that cup over 80 on the sensory scale (see Cupping), regarded for their unique individual characteristics. They are usually traded outside of the commodities market in small batches, resulting in wider availability of quality coffees.

Specialty/speciality

interchangeable in this context, U.S. English and U.K. English respectively.

Torrefacto

sugar-roasted beans common in Southeast Asia, Spain, and Latin America. The beans are sometimes coated in margarine or butter, too. Also known as a *kopi* roast or *café torrado.*

SOURCES AND READINGS

Introduction

Fairtrade Foundation: *About Coffee.* www.fairtrade.org.uk/farmers-and-workers/coffee/about-coffee (accessed 26 May 2021).

Saint-Pierre, Bernardin de: *A Voyage to the Isle of Mauritius, (or, Isle of France), the Isle of Bourbon, and the Cape of Good Hope: With Observations and Reflections Upon Nature and Mankind by a French Officer.* Griffin, 1775.

Tanzania Coffee Association: *Tanzania Coffee Industry. Development Strategy 2011/2021.* Tanzania Coffee Board (2012, July 24), www.coffeeboard.or.tz/News_publications/startegy_english.pdf (accessed 26 May 2021).

Basics

Cole, Nicki Lisa, and Keith Brown: *The Problem with Fair Trade Coffee.* Contexts, vol. 13, no. 1, Feb. 2014, pp. 50–55, DOI: 10.1177/1536504214522009. (accessed 11 June 2021).

Fairtrade Foundation: *About Coffee.* www.fairtrade.org.uk/farmers-and-workers/coffee/about-coffee (accessed 10 June 2021).

Haight, Colleen: *The Problem With Fair Trade Coffee.* Stanford Social Innovation Review, Stanford University, 2011, ssir.org/articles/entry/the_problem_with_fair_trade_coffee (accessed 11 June 2021).

Kingston, Lani: *How to Make Coffee: The Science Behind the Bean.* Abrams, 2015.

Seeds of Change

Ukers, William Harrison: *All About Coffee.* Tea and Coffee Trade Journal Company, New York, 1922, p. 125.

Arabian Peninsula

Abu Dhabi Culture, Department of Culture and Tourism: *Gahwa.* 18 Dec. 2018, abudhabiculture.ae/en/unesco/intangible-cultural-heritage/gahwa (accessed 1 June 2021).

Arendonk, C. Van, and Chaudhuri, K.N.: *Ḳahwa.* In: *Encyclopaedia of Islam,* edited by P. Bearman, Th. Bianquis, C.E. Bosworth, E. van Donzel, W.P. Heinrichs. DOI: 10.1163/1573-3912_islam_COM_0418 (accessed 31 May 2021).

Campo, Juan Eduardo: *Encyclopedia of Islam.* Facts On File, 2009, p. 155.

Ellis, Markman: *The Coffee-House: A Cultural History.* Orion, 2011.

Hattox, Ralph S.: *Coffee and Coffeehouses: The Origins of a Social Beverage in the Medieval Near East.* University of Washington Press, 1985.

Keatinge, Margaret Clark, and Khayat, Marie Karam: *Food from the Arab World.* Khayats, 1965, p. 141.

Kiple, Kenneth F., and Coneè Ornelas, Kriemhild (Eds.): The Cambridge World History of Food. Cambridge University Press, 2000, p. 1143.

Sowayan, Saad Abdullah: *Nabati Poetry: The Oral Poetry of Arabia.* University of California Press, 1985.

Weinberg, Bennett Alan, and Bealer, Bonnie K.: *The World of Caffeine: The Science and Culture of the World's Most Popular Drug.* Routledge, 2001, p. 12.

Austria, Germany, Switzerland

Ferguson, M.: *How is coffee decaffeinated? A brief history and overview of methodologies.* 29. Nov. 2020, olamspecialtycoffee.com/blog/how-is-coffee-decaffeinated-a-brief-history.html (accessed 15 April 2022).

Heim, G.: *Swiss history – the invention of coffee without the pot.* 28. Sept. 2021, blog.nationalmuseum.ch/en/2018/10/history-of-coffee-the-invention-of-nescafe/ (accessed 15 April 2022).

Kapeller, S.: *Quirks of Viennese cuisine.* Wien Info, wien.info/en/shopping-wining-dining/viennese-cuisine/quirks-of-viennese-cuisine-356154 (accessed 14 April 2022).

Liberles, R.: *Jews welcome coffee: Tradition and innovation in early Modern Germany.* Brandeis Univ. Press, 2012, (pp. 27, 29).

Melitta: *Melitta® - Our Passion through the years.* melitta.com/en/Our-Passion-through-the-Years-628.html (accessed 15 April 2022).

Nestlé: *What did we do when the bank called? Invented Nescafé.* nestle.com/aboutus/history/nestle-company-history/nescafe (accessed 15 April 2022).

Nestlé UK: *HISTORY OF INSTANT COFFEE.* 2008, web.archive.org/web/20080221181504/http://www.nestle.co.uk/OurBrands/AboutOurBrands/Beverages/History+of+Instant+Coffee.htm (accessed 15 April 2022).

Oberzill, Gerhard H.: *Ins Kaffeehaus!: Geschichte einer Wiener Institution.* Jugend & Volk Verlage, 1983, pp. 77–85.

Oldenburg, R.: *The Great Good Place: Cafés, coffee shops, community centers, beauty parlors, general stores, bars, hangouts, and how they get you through the day.* Marlowe, 1997.

Österreichische UNESCO-Kommission: *Viennese Coffee House.* 2011, Culture.unesco.at/en/culture/intangible-cultural-heritage/national-inventory/news-1/article/viennese-coffee-house-culture (accessed 4 April 2022).

Polgar, A.: *Theorie des "Café Central."* In H. B. Segel: The Vienna Coffeehouse Wits, 1890-1938, Purdue University Press, 1995, pp. 267-270.

Unowsky, D.: *Stimulating Culture: Coffee and Coffeehouses in Modern European History.* Journal of Urban History, 42(4), 2016, S. 806–810. DOI: 10.1177/0096144216645780 (accessed 4 April 2022).

Walker, A.: 1913: *When Hitler, Trotsky, Tito, Freud and Stalin all lived in the same place.* 17. April 2013, bbc.com/news/magazine-21859771 (accessed 4 April 2022).

Zloczower, G., Moss, J.: *13 different kinds of coffee found in Vienna's coffeehouses.* Vienna Würstelstand, 26. Sept. 2020, viennawurstelstand.com/article/13-different-kinds-of-coffee-found-in-viennas-coffeehouses/ (accessed 14 April 2022).

Brazil

Armstrong, Martin, and Richter, Felix: *The Countries Most Addicted to Coffee.* Statista Infographics, 01 Oct. 2020, www.statista.com/chart/8602/top-coffee-drinking-nations (accessed 07 June 2021).

Campbell, Dawn, and Smith, Janet L.: *The Coffee Book.* Pelican Publishing Company, 1993, p. 76.

Coffee Consumption and Industry Strategies in Brazil. A Volume in the Consumer Science and Strategic Marketing Series, Elsevier Science, 2019, p. 259.

Coffee Report 2020 Statista Consumer Market Outlook—Segment Report. Statista, 2020, www.statista.com/study/48823/coffee-report (accessed 7 June 2021)

Cole, Allan B.: *Japan's Population Problems in War and Peace.* Pacific Affairs, vol. 16, no. 4, 1943, pp. 397–417, JSTOR, www.jstor.org/stable/2752077 (accessed 8 June 2021).

De Bivar Marquese, Rafael: *African Diaspora, Slavery, and the Paraiba Valley Coffee Plantation Landscape: Nineteenth-Century Brazil.* Review (Fernand Braudel Center), vol. 31, no. 2, 2008, pp. 195–216, JSTOR, www.jstor.org/stable/40241714 (accessed 4 June 2021).

Dicum, Gregory, and Luttinger, Nina: *The Coffee Book: Anatomy of an Industry from Crop to the Last Drop.* New Press, 2012.

Engerman, Stanley L.: *The Abolition of the Atlantic Slave Trade: Origins and Effects in Europe, Africa, and the Americas.* University of Wisconsin Press, 1981, p. 291.

Engines in Brazil Use Coffee As Fuel. Popular Science Monthly, vol. 120, no. 4, Apr. 1932, p. 30.

Fridell, Gavin: *Coffee and the Capitalist Market. Fair Trade Coffee: The Prospects and Pitfalls of Market-driven Social Justice.* University of Toronto, 2008, pp. 101–34.

Gas from the Low-Grade Coffee. The Canberra Times, 29 December 1932, nla.gov.au/nla.news-article2326815 (accessed 7 June 2021).

Hutchinson, Lincoln: *Coffee 'Valorization' in Brazil.* The Quarterly Journal of Economics, vol. 23, no. 3, 1909, pp. 528–535, JSTOR, www.jstor.org/stable/1884777 (accessed 4 June 2021).

Jacobowitz, Seth: *A Bitter Brew: Coffee and Labor in Japanese Brazilian Immigrant Literature.* Estudos Japoneses 41, pp. 13–30.

Minahan, James: *Ethnic Groups of North, East, and Central Asia: An Encyclopedia.* ABC-CLIO, 2014, p. 59.

Nishida, Mieko: *Diaspora and Identity: Japanese Brazilians in Brazil and Japan.* University of Hawaii Press, 2017.

Ottanelli, Fraser M., et al.: *Italian Workers of the World: Labor Migration and the Formation of Multiethnic States.* University of Illinois Press, 2001, p. 103.

Richard, Christopher: Brazil. Marshall Cavendish, 1991.

Topik, Steven: *The World Coffee Market in the eighteenth and nineteenth Centuries, from Colonial to National Regimes.* Working Papers of the Global Economic History Network (GEHN) (04/04), Department of Economic History, London School of Economics and Political Science, 2004.

Volsi, Bruno et al.: *The Dynamics of Coffee Production in Brazil.* PloS one, 23 July 2019, DOI:10.1371/journal.pone.0219742 (accessed 5 June 2021).

Woodyard, George, and Vincent, Jon S.: *Culture and Customs of Brazil.* Greenwood Press, 2003. p. 85.

Ethiopia

Barker, William C., et al.: *First Footsteps in East Africa, Or, An Exploration of Harar.* Tylston and Edwards, 1894, p. 34.

Bruce, James: *Travels to Discover the Source of the Nile, in the Years 1768, 1769, 1770, 1771, 1772, and 1773.* Vol II, G.G.J. and J. Robinson, 1790.

Duressa, Endalkachew Lelisa: *The Socio-Cultural Aspects of Coffee Production in Southwestern Ethiopia: An Overview.* Journal of Culture, Society and Development, vol. 38, 2018, p. 15.

Éloi Ficquet: *Coffee in Ethiopia: History, Culture and Challenges,* edited by Siegbert Uhlig, David Appleyard, Alessandro Bausi, Wolfgang Hahn, Steven Kaplan, Michigan State Press, 2018, pp. 155–160.

Farley, David: Discovering the Birthplace of Coffee in Ethiopia, Afar, May 2013, www.afar.com/magazine/coffeeland (accessed 27 April 2021).

Haile-Mariam, Teketel: *The Production, Marketing, and Economic Impact of Coffee in Ethiopia.* Stanford University, 1973 as quoted in *Coffee: A Comprehensive Guide to the Bean, the Beverage, and the Industry,* edited by Robert W. Thurston, Jonathan Morris, Shawn Steiman, Rowman & Littlefield, 2013, p. 153.

Harris, William Cornwallis, Sir: *The Highlands of Æthiopia.* Longman, Brown, Green, and Longmans, 1844.

Mace, Pascal Mawuli: *A la découverte de l'Ethiopie, Addis Abeba. Rencontre avec la famille impériale.* 2020, p. 18.

Montagnon, C., Mahyoub, A., Solano, W., & Sheibani, F.: *Unveiling a Unique Genetic Diversity of Cultivated Coffea Arabica L. in its Main Domestication Center: Yemen.* Genetic Resources and Crop Evolution, 2021, link.springer.com/article/10.1007/s10722-021-01139-y (accessed 27 April 2021).

Wane, Njoki Nathani: *Gender, Democracy and Institutional Development in Africa.* Palgrave Macmillan, 2019, p. 175.

India

Aggarwal, Ramesh Kumar, et al.: *Coffee Industry in India: Production to Consumption—A Sustainable Enterprise.* Coffee in Health and Disease Prevention, edited by Victor Preedy, Academic Press, 2014, pp. 61–70.

Bhattacharya, Bhaswati: *Local History of a Global Commodity: Production of Coffee in Mysore and Coorg in the Nineteenth Century.* Indian Historical Review, 41(1), 2014, pp. 67–86.

Bhattacharya, Bhaswati: *Much Ado Over Coffee: Indian Coffee House Then And Now.* Routledge, 2017.

Blake, Stephen P.: *Shahjahanabad: The Sovereign City in Mughal India,1639–1739.* Cambridge University Press, 1991.

Coffee Industry and Exports. IBEF, www.ibef.org/exports/coffee-industry-in-india.aspx (accessed 21 May 2021).

Crooke, William. *Things Indian: Being Discursive Notes on Various Subjects Connected with India.* J. Murray, 1906, p. 108.

Edward A. Alpers, Chhaya Goswami: *Transregional Trade and Traders: Situating Gujarat in the Indian Ocean from Early Times to 1900.* Oxford University Press, 2019.

Gotthold, Julia J., and Gotthold, Donald W. *Indian Ocean.* Clio Press, 1988, p. xvii.

Indian Coffee Board. Government of India, www.indiacoffee.org/aboutus.aspx (accessed 7 April 2021).

Jain, V. K.: *The Role of the Arab Traders in Western India During the Early Medieval Period.* Proceedings of the Indian History Congress, vol. 39, 1978, pp. 285–295.

Krishan, Shubhra: *When Indian Coffee House was the Country's Living Room.* Condé Nast Traveller, 22 September 2016, www.cntraveller.in/story/when-indian-coffee-house-was-the-countrys-living-room (accessed 7 April 2021).

Maloni, Ruby Maloni: *Straddling the Arabian Sea: Gujarati Trade with West Asia 17th and 18th Centuries.* Proceedings of the Indian History Congress, vol. 64, 2003, pp. 622–636.

Naidu, Sasubilli Paradesi: *Coffee Industry in India—A Historical Perspective.* IOSR Journal Of Humanities And Social Science (IOSR-JHSS), vol. 23, issue 8, ver. 4, August 2018, www.iosrjournals.org/iosr-jhss/papers/Vol.%2023%20Issue8/Version-4/D2308042933.pdf (accessed 21 May 2021).

Preedy, Victor: *Coffee in Health and Disease Prevention.* Elsevier Science, 2014, p. 62.

Saravanan, Velayutham, and Islamia, Jamia Millia: *Colonialism and Coffee Plantations: Decline of Environment and Tribals in Madras Presidency During the Nineteenth Century.* Indian Economic & Social History Review 41(4), December 2004.

Seland, E.: *Networks and Social Cohesion in Ancient Indian Ocean Trade: Geography, Ethnicity, Religion.* Journal of Global History, 8(3), 2013, pp. 373–390, DOI:10.1017/S1740022813000338 (accessed 20 May 2021).

Spuler, Bertold: *The Muslim World: The Last Great Muslim Empires.* Brill, 1969, p. 61.

Thakur, Sankarshan: *The Brothers Bihari.* Harper Collins, 2015.

Cardamom Market. Mordor Intelligence, www.mordorintelligence.com/industry-reports/cardamom-market (accessed 7 April 2021).

Indonesia

Cramer, P. J. S.: *A Review of Literature of Coffee Research in Indonesia.* Inter-American Institute of Agricultural Science, 1957, pp. 45, 177.

Dell, Melissa, and Olken, Benjamin A.: *The Development Effects Of The Extractive Colonial Economy: The Dutch Cultivation System In Java.* Harvard University and MIT, October 2018, p. 13.

Farah, Adriana (ed.): *Production, Quality and Chemistry.* Royal Society of Chemistry, 2019, p. 79.

Gordon, Alec: *Indonesia, Plantations and the "Post-Colonial" Mode of Production.* Journal of Contemporary Asia, 12:2, 1982, pp. 168–187, DOI: 10.1080/00472338285390141 (accessed 21 May 2021).

Hidayah, Zulyani: *A Guide to Tribes in Indonesia: Anthropological Insights from the Archipelago.* Springer Singapore, 2020, p. 219.

Haswidi, Andi, and BEKRAF: *Kopi: Indonesian Coffee Craft & Culture.* Afterhours Books, 2017.

History of Coffee. National Coffee Association of U. S. A., www.ncausa.org/about-coffee/history-of-coffee (accessed 09 May 2021)

Kusama, Ellen: Ngelelet: *Ketika Eksistensi Rokok Tidak Menyebalkan.* 16 December 2016, kesengsemlasem.com/ngelelet-momen-ketika-eksistensi-rokok-tidak-menyebalkan (accessed 21 May 2021).

Lucas, John A.: *Fungi, Food Crops, and Biosecurity: Advances and Challenges.* Advances in Food Security and Sustainability, 2017.

Multatuli: *Max Havelaar, or, the Coffee Auctions of the Dutch Trading Company.* New York Review Books, 2019.

Nafis, Anas, et al.: *Peribahasa Minangkabau.* Intermasa, 1996, p. 223.

Ricklefs, M. C.: *A History of Modern Indonesia since c. 1200.* Macmillan, 2001, p. 156.

Soerodjo, Irawan: *The Advancement of Land Law in Indonesia.* Journal of Law, Policy and Globalization, vol. 37, 2015, pp. 198–203.

Van Nederveen Meerkerk, Elise: *Women, Work and Colonialism in the Netherlands and Java: Comparisons, Contrasts, and Connections, 1830–1940.* Springer International Publishing, 2019, p. 93.

Vega, Fernando E.: *The Rise of Coffee.* American Scientist, vol. 96, no. 2, March/April 2008, p. 138.

Wisudawan, Adhitya Pramudia: *The Production and the Consumption of 'Nyethe' in Tulungagung.* Allusion, vol. 02, no. 02, August 2013, journal.unair.ac.id/download-fullpapers-allusionfc701fe8adfull.pdf (accessed 21 May 2021).

Italy

A Gourmet Expoforum Fipe Racconta Il Bar Italiano. Federazione Italiana Pubblici Exercizi, 11 June 2018, www.fipe.it/comunicazione/note-per-la-stampa/item/5768-a-gourmet-expoforum-fipe-racconta-il-bar-italiano.html (accessed 14 June 2021).

Bersten, Ian: *Coffee Floats Tea Sinks: Through History and Technology to a Complete Understanding.* Helian Books, 1993.

Caprino, Edoardo, and Vecchio, Mauro: *COFFEE MONITOR: 260 Euro La Spesa Media Annua Degli Italiani Per Il Caffè.* Nomisma—Datalytics, 2018, nomisma.it/wp-content/uploads/2019/11/COFFEE_MONITOR_NOMISMA.pdf (accessed 14 June 2021).

Crocco, Eloisa: *Neapolitan Express: Il Caffè.* Rogiosi, 2016.

Halevy, Alon: *The Infinite Emotions of Coffee.* Macchiatone Communications, 2011, p. 62.

Hinds, Kathryn: *Venice and Its Merchant Empire.* Benchmark Books, 2002.

Johnson-Laird, Philip Nicholas: *How We Reason.* Oxford University Press, 2006, p. 174.

Lima, Darcy R., and Santos, Roseane M.: *An Unashamed Defense of Coffee.* Xlibris Corporation LLC, 2009.

Marocchino Coffee: History and Recipe—Espresso Laboratory. Laboratorio Dell'espresso, 17 July 2018. laboratorioespresso.it/en/marocchino-coffee-recipe (accessed 13 June 2021).

Parasecoli, Fabio: *Food Culture in Italy.* Greenwood Press, 2004, p. 128.

Stull, Eric, et al.: *The History of Coffee in Guatemala.* Independent Publishing Group, 2001.

Ukers, William Harrison. *All About Coffee.* Tea and Coffee Trade Journal Company, 1922.

Japan

珍版横浜文明開化語辞典: 舶来語と漢字の出会い「宛字」集. Japan, 光画コミュニケーションプロダクツ, 2007, p. 38.

淹れる・選ぶ・楽しむコーヒーのある暮らし (池田書店). N. p., 株式会社ＰＨＰ研究所, 2020, p. 22.

Amiami: 炭火焙煎したコーヒーの特徴. Coffeemecca, 26 Sept. 2016, coffeemecca.jp/column/trivia/7850 (accessed 08 June 2021).

Brown, Kendall H., and Minichiello, Sharon: *Taishō Chic: Japanese Modernity, Nostalgia, and Deco.* Honolulu Academy of Arts, 2001.

Buckley, Sandra: *Encyclopedia of Contemporary Japanese Culture.* Routledge, 2009, p. 79.

Callow, Chloë: *Cold Brew Coffee: Techniques, Recipes & Cocktails for Coffee's Hottest Trend.* Octopus, 2017.

Coffee Market in Japan. All Japan Coffee Association, July 2012, coffee.ajca.or.jp/wp-content/uploads/2012/07/coffee_market_in_japan.pdf (accessed 08 June 2021).

Cole, Allan B.: *Japan's Population Problems in War and Peace.* Pacific Affairs, vol. 16, no. 4, 1943, pp. 397–417, JSTOR, www.jstor.org/stable/2752077 (accessed 8 June 2021).

Diep, C.: *Total Coffee Consumption in Japan from 1990 to 2019.* Statista Infographics, 04 March 2021, www.statista.com/statistics/314986/japan-total-coffee-consumption (accessed 07 June 2021).

Felton, Emma. Filtered: *Coffee, the Café and the 21st-Century City.* Taylor & Francis, 2018.

Freeman, James, Caitlin Freeman, Tara Duggan, Clay McLachlan, and Michelle Ott: *The Blue Bottle Craft of Coffee: Growing, Roasting, and Drinking, with Recipes.* Ten Speed, 2012, p. 88.

Leavenworth, J. Lynn, and Aikawa, Takaaki. *The Mind of Japan; a Christian Perspective.* Judson Press, 1967, p. 105.

Lone, S.: *The Japanese Community in Brazil, 1908–1940: Between Samurai and Carnival.* Palgrave Macmillan UK, 2001.

Mackintosh, Michelle, and Wide, Steve: *Tokyo.* Pan Macmillan Australia, 2018, p. 140.

Masterson, Daniel M., and Funada-Classen, Sayaka: *The Japanese in Latin America.* University of Illinois Press, 2004.

Minahan, James: *Ethnic Groups of North, East, and Central Asia: An Encyclopedia.* ABC-CLIO, 2014, p. 59.

Namba, Tsuneo, and Matsuse, Tomoco: *[A historical study of coffee in Japanese and Asian countries: focusing the medicinal uses in Asian traditional medicines].* Yakushigaku zasshi, vol. 37,1, 2002, pp. 65–75.

Niehaus, Andreas, and Walravens, Tina (eds.): *Feeding Japan: The Cultural and Political Issues of Dependency and Risk.* Springer International Publishing, 2017, p. 182.

O'Dwyer, Emer Sinéad: *Significant Soil: Settler Colonialism and Japan's Urban Empire in Manchuria.* Harvard U Asia Center, 2015, p. 49.

Rosa, David: *The Artisan Roaster: The Complete Guide to Setting Up Your Own Coffee Roastery Cafe.* Amazon Digital Services LLC – KDP Print US, 2020.

Shurtleff, William, and Aoyagi, Akiko: *History of Soynuts, Soynut Butter, Japanese-Style Roasted Soybeans (Irimame) and Setsubun (with Mamemaki) (1068–2012).* Soyinfo Center, 2012, p. 77.

Suzuki, Teiiti: *The Japanese Immigrant in Brazil.* University of Tokyo Press, 1969, p. 12.

White, Merry: *Coffee Life in Japan.* University of California Press, 2012, pp. 66, 96, 100.

Yoshikawa, Muneo, and Hijirida, Kyoko: *Japanese Language and Culture for Business and Travel.* University of Hawaii Press, 1987, p. 115.

Korea

BAE, Jung Sook: *Consumer Advertising for Korean Women and Impacts of Early Consumer Products under Japanese Colonial Rule.* Icon, vol. 18, 2012, pp. 104–121. JSTOR, www.jstor.org/stable/23789343 (accessed 15 April 2021).

Griffis, William Elliot: *Corea, the Hermit Nation.* Cambridge University Press, 2014.

Hundt, David, and Bleiker, Roland: *Reconciling Colonial Memories in Korea and Japan.* Asian Perspective, vol. 31, no. 1, special issue on "Reconciliation between China and Japan," The Johns Hopkins University Press, 2007, pp. 61–91.

Lancaster, William Scott, and Sun, Jiaming: *Chinese Globalization: A Profile of People-based Global Connections in China.* Routledge, 2013, p. 126.

Lowell, Percival: *Chosōn, the Land of the Morning Calm; a Sketch of Korea.* Boston, Ticknor and Company, 1886.

Park, Young-soon: 커피인문학. *Coffee Humanities. How did Coffee Seduce the World?,* 2017.

Sangmee, Bak: *Reinventing Korean Food: National Taste and Globalization—From Strange Bitter Concoction to Romantic Necessity: The Social History of Coffee Drinking in South Korea.* Korea Journal 45/2, 2005.

Williams, LT. COL. Alex N.: *Subsistence Supply in Korea.* Q. M. C Quartermaster Review, January-February 1953.

Mexico

Alexander, William L., et al: *Neoliberalism and Commodity Production in Mexico.* University Press of Colorado, 2012.

Gliessman, Stephen R., and Rosemeyer, Martha: *The Conversion to Sustainable Agriculture: Principles, Processes and Practices.* CRC Press, 2010.

Jaffee, Daniel: *Brewing Justice: Fair Trade Coffee, Sustainability, and Survival.* University of California Press, 2014, p. 38.

Kennedy, Diana: *The Essential Cuisines of Mexico.* Clarkson Potter, 2009.

Long, Long Towell, et al.: *Food Culture in Mexico.* Greenwood Press, 2005, p. 21.

Martinez-Torres, Maria Elena: *Survival Strategies in Neoliberal Markets: Peasant Organizations and Organic Coffee in Chiapas.* in: Mexico in Transition: Neoliberal Globalism, the State and Civil Society, by Gerardo Otero, Fernwood Publ., 2007.

Nolan-Ferrell, Catherine: *Agrarian Reform and Revolutionary Justice in Soconusco, Chiapas: Campesinos and the Mexican State, 1934–1940.* Journal of Latin American Studies, vol. 42, no. 3, 2010, pp. 551–585. JSTOR, www.jstor.org/stable/40984895 (accessed 11 June 2021).

Otera, Adriana: *Coffee Annual: Mexico.* US Department of Agriculture, Foreign Agricultural Service, May 2021, apps.fas.usda.gov/newgainapi/api/Report/DownloadReportByFileName?fileName=Coffee+Annual_Mexico+City_Mexico_05-15-2021.pdf (accessed 11 June 2021).

Perfecto, Ivette, et al.: *Coffee Landscapes Shaping the Anthropocene: Forced Simplification on a Complex Agroecological Landscape.* Current Anthropology, vol. 60, no. S20, Aug. 2019, DOI:10.1086/703413. (accessed 11 June 2021).

Renard, Marie-Christine, and Breña, Mariana Ortega: *The Mexican Coffee Crisis.* Latin American Perspectives, vol. 37, no. 2, 2010, pp. 21–33, JSTOR, www.jstor.org/stable/20684713 (accessed 11 June 2021).

Robertiello, Jack: *Drinking in the Flavors of Mexico.* Américas, vol. 46–47, Organization of American States, 1994, p. 58.

Shapiro, Howard-Yana, and Grivetti, Louis E.: *Chocolate: History, Culture, and Heritage.* Wiley, 2011.

Simposium Política Mexicana: *Mexico.* Sociedad Mexicana de Geografía y Estadística, 1970.

Ukers, William Harrison. *All About Coffee.* Tea and Coffee Trade Journal Company, 1922, p. 221.

Polynesia

Crawford, J.C.: *On New Zealand Coffee.* In: *Transactions of the Royal Society of New Zealand,* ed. by J. Hector, vol. 9, Royal Society of New Zealand, 1877, pp. 545–546.

Kinro, Gerald: *A Cup of Aloha: The Kona Coffee Epic.* University of Hawai'i Press, 2003.

Landcare Research Manaki Whenua: *Plant Use Details of Coprosma robusta.* Māori Plant Use Database, Ngā Tipu Whakaoranga Database, 2021, maoriplantuse.landcareresearch.co.nz, Record ID Number 1140 (accessed 23 May 2021).

McLintock, A.H. (ed.): *Crawford, James Coutts.* In: *An Encyclopaedia of New Zealand,* Te Ara—the Encyclopedia of New Zealand, 1966, www.TeAra.govt.nz/en/1966/crawford-james-coutts (accessed 24 May 2021).

Melillo, Edward D.: *Boki's Beans: A People's History of Hawaiian Coffee.* Honolulu Magazine, 27 May 2021, www.honolulumagazine.com/bokis-beans-a-peoples-history-of-hawaiian-coffee (accessed 15 June 2021).

Roberts, Peter, and Trewick, Chad: *Specialty Coffee Transaction Guide 2020.* 2020, www.transactionguide.coffee (accessed 27 May 2021).

Schmitt, Robert C., and Ronck, Ronn: *Firsts and Almost Firsts in Hawai'i.* University of Hawai'i Press, 1995, p. 17.

Stanley, David: *South Pacific Handbook.* Moon Publications, 1993, p. 126.

State of Hawaii Department of Agriculture Market Analysis and News Branch, et al.: *Coffee Acreage, Yield, Production, Price and Value State of Hawaii, 2020.* May 2020, hdoa.hawaii.gov/add/files/2020/06/Coffee-Stats-2019_SOH-05.29.20.pdf (accessed 27 May 2021).

Tahiti Tourisme: *Tahiti Dining Fact Sheets.* The Islands of Tahiti, 20 May 2020, tahititourisme.com/en-us/media/fact-sheets/dining (accessed 23 May 2021).

Singapore

Bernards, Brian C.: *Writing the South Seas: Imagining the Nanyang in Chinese and Southeast Asian Postcolonial Literature.* University of Washington Press, 2015.

Chang, Cheryl, and McGonigle, Ian: *Kopi Culture: Consumption, Conservatism and Cosmopolitanism among Singapore's Millennials.* Asian Anthropology, 19:3, 2020, pp. 213–231, DOI: 10.1080/1683478X.2020.1726965 (accessed 20 May 2021).

Eng, Lai Ah: The Kopitiam in Singapore: *An Evolving about Migration and Cultural Diversity.* Asia Research Institute Working Paper No. 132, 2010, papers.ssrn.com/sol3/papers.cfm?abstract_id=1716534 (accessed 7 April 2021).

Vaughan, J.D. Vaughan: *The Manners and Customs of the Chinese of the Straits Settlements.* Mission Press, 1879

Yap, M.T.: *Hainanese in the Restaurant and Catering Business.* In: *Chinese Dialect Groups: Traits and Trades,* ed. by T.T.W. Tan, Opinion Books, 1990, pp. 78–79.

Spain

Burdett, Avani: *Delicatessen Cookbook—Burdett's Delicatessen Recipes: How to make and sell Continental & World Cuisine foods.* Springwood emedia, 2012.

Campbell, Jodi: *At the First Table: Food and Social Identity in Early Modern Spain.* University of Nebraska Press, 2017.

Foreign Crops and Markets. The Bureau, 1947, p. 208.

Fowler-Salamini, Heather: *Working Women, Entrepreneurs, and the Mexican Revolution: The Coffee Culture of Córdoba, Veracruz.* University of Nebraska Press, 2013.

Hempstead, William H., et al.: *The History of Coffee in Guatemala.* Independent Publishing Group, 2001.

Imamuddin, S.M.: *Muslim Spain 711–1492 A.D.: A Sociological Study.* Brill, 1981.

Kurlansky, Mark: *Milk! A 10,000-Year Food Fracas.* Bloomsbury Publishing, 2018.

Preedy, Victor: *Coffee in Health and Disease Prevention.* Elsevier Science, 2014, p. 90.

Terry, Laurence M.: *Coffee Culture in Mexico.* Comp. Frederick Marriott, The Overland Monthly 37, 1901, pp. 703–09.

Ukers, William Harrison. *All About Coffee.* Tea and Coffee Trade Journal Company, 1922, pp. 241, 686.

Vega, César et al.: *The Kitchen as Laboratory: Reflections on the Science of Food and Cooking.* Columbia University Press, 2013, p. 94.

Willson, Anthony: *Equatorial Guinea Political History, and Governance, the Hidden History.* Lulu.com, 2017.

Tanzania

Ashkenazi, Michael, and Jacob, Jeanne: *The World Cookbook: The Greatest Recipes from Around the Globe.* ABC-CLIO, 2014, p. 144.

Charles, Goodluck, and Anderson, Wineaster: *International Marketing: Theory and Practice from Developing Countries.* Cambridge Scholars Publishing, 2016, p. 6.

Davis, Aaron & Govaerts, Rafaël & fls, DIANE & Stoffelen, Piet.: *An annotated taxonomic conspectus of genus Coffea (Rubiaceae).* Botanical Journal of the Linnean Society, 152, 2006, pp. 465–512, DOI: 10.1111/j.1095-8339.2006.00584.x. (accessed 5 May 2021).

Haustein, Jörg: *Strategic Tangles: Slavery, Colonial Policy, and Religion in German East Africa, 1885–1918.* Atlantic Studies, 14:4, 2017, pp. 497–518, DOI: 10.1080/14788810.2017.1300753 (accessed 10 May 2021).

Kieran, J.A.: *The Origins of Commercial Arabica Coffee Production in East Africa.* African Historical Studies, vol. 2, no. 1, Boston University African Studies Center, 1969, pp. 51–67. DOI: 10.2307/216326 (accessed 21 May 2021).

Kourampas N., Shipton C., et al.: *Late Quaternary Speleogenesis and Landscape Evolution in a Tropical Carbonate Island: Pango la Kuumbi (Kuumbi Cave), Zanzibar.* International Journal of Speleology, 44 (3), 2015, pp. 293–314. DOI: 10.5038/1827-806X.44.3.7 (accessed 9 May 2021).

Maganda, Dainess Mashiku: *Swahili People and Their Language.* Adonis & Abbey, 2014, p. 74.

Munger, Edwin S.: *African Coffee on Kilimanjaro: A Chagga Kihamba.* Economic Geography, vol. 28, no. 2, 1952, pp. 181–185, JSTOR, www.jstor.org/stable/141027 (accessed 27 May 2021).

Sheriff, Abdul: *Slaves, Spices, and Ivory in Zanzibar: Integration of an East African Commercial Empire into the World Economy, 1770–1873.* Eastern African Studies, Ohio University Press, 1987.

Smallholder Farming and Smallholder Development in Tanzania: Ten Case Studies. Weltforum Verlag, 1968, p. 177.

Soini, E.: *Changing Livelihoods on the Slopes of Mt. Kilimanjaro, Tanzania: Challenges and Opportunities in the Chagga Homegarden System.* Agroforest Syst 64, 2005, pp. 157–167, DOI: 10.1007/s10457-004-1023-y (accessed 27 May 2021).

Thomas, A.S.: *Types of Robusta Coffee and their Selection in Uganda.* The East African Agricultural Journal, 1:3, 1935, pp. 193–197, DOI: 10.1080/03670074.1935.11663646 (accessed 21 May 2021).

Tripp, Aili Mari: *Changing the Rules: The Politics of Liberalization and the Urban Informal Economy in Tanzania.* University of California Press, 1997, p.33.

Weiss, Brad: *Sacred Trees, Bitter Harvests: Globalizing Coffee in Northwest Tanzania.* University of Michigan, 2003, p. 18.

Wood, M., Panighello, S., Orsega, E.F. et al.: *Zanzibar and Indian Ocean trade in the first Millennium CE: the Glass Bead Evidence.* Archaeol Anthropol Sci 9, 2017, pp. 879–901, DOI: 10.1007/s12520-015-0310-z (accessed 10 May 2021).

The Caribbean

Adler, Leonore Loeb, and Uwe p. Gielen: *Migration: Immigration and Emigration in International Perspective.* Praeger, 2003, p. 124.

Bryan, Patrick E.: *The Haitian Revolution and Its Effects.* Taylor & Francis Group, 1984, p. 33.

Corbett, Ben: *This Is Cuba: An Outlaw Culture Survives.* Basic Books, 2007.

Daily Consular and Trade Reports No. 3174. U.S. Government Printing Office, 12 May 1908, p. 5.

Daly, Jack & Hamrick, Danny & Fernandez-Stark, Karina & Bamber, Penny: *Jamaica in the Arabica Coffee Global Value Chain.* 2018, DOI: 10.13140/RG.2.2.35977.95849 (accessed 10 June 2021).

DeMers, John: *Food of Jamaica: Authentic Recipes from the Jewel of the Caribbean.* Tuttle Publishing, 1998, p. 23.

Dicum, Gregory, and Luttinger, Nina: *The Coffee Book: Anatomy of an Industry from Crop to the Last Drop.* New Press, 2012.

Fatah-Black, Karwan: *White Lies and Black Markets: Evading Metropolitan Authority in Colonial Suriname, 1650–1800.* Brill, 2015, p. 69.

Figueredo, D.H., and Argote-Freyre, Frank: *A Brief History of the Caribbean.* Facts On File, Incorporated, 2008, p. xvi.

Head, David (ed.): *Encyclopedia of the Atlantic World, 1400–1900: Europe, Africa, and the Americas in An Age of Exploration, Trade, and Empires [2 Volumes].* ABC-CLIO, 2017, p. 571.

History of Coffee. National Coffee Association of U.S.A., www.ncausa.org/about-coffee/history-of-coffee (accessed 09 May 2021)

Kirk, John M., and Halebsky, Sandor: *Cuba- twenty-five Years of Revolution, 1959–1984.* Praeger, 1985, p. 70.

Klein, Herbert S.: *African Slavery in Latin America and the Caribbean.* Oxford University Press, 25 Sep 1986.

Lawson, George, and Go, Julian (eds.): *Global Historical Sociology.* Cambridge University Press, 2017, p. 77.

Morris, Jonathan: *Coffee: A Global History.* Reaktion Books, 2018.

Newburry, William: *The Caribbean.* The Sage Encyclopedia of Corporate Reputation (ed. Craig E. Carroll), Thousand Oaks: Sage, 2016.

Pérez, Louis A.: *Cuba: Between Reform and Revolution.* Oxford University Press, 2015, pp. 82, 286.

Popkin, Jeremy D.: *You Are All Free: The Haitian Revolution and the Abolition of Slavery.* Cambridge University Press, 2010.

Trouillot, Michel-Rolph: *Motion in the System: Coffee, Color, and Slavery in Eighteenth-Century Saint-Domingue.* Review (Fernand Braudel Center), vol. 5, no. 3, 1982, pp. 331–388. JSTOR, www.jstor.org/stable/40240909 (accessed 9 June 2021).

Schroeder, Kira: *The Case of Blue Mountain Coffee, Jamaica.* In: *Guide to Geographical Indications: Linking Products and Their Origins,* by Daniele Giovannucci, International Trade Centre, 2009, pp. 170–76.

Sheen, Barbara: *Foods of Cuba.* Greenhaven Publishing LLC, 2010.

Siegel, P., and Alwang, J.R.: *Export commodity production and broad-based rural development: coffee and cocoa in the Dominican Republic.* World Bank, Agriculture and Rural Development Dept. and Latin American and the Caribbean Region, Rural Development Family, 2004, p. 36.

Terry, Thomas Philip: *Terry's Guide to Cuba: Including the Isle of Pinea, with a Chapter on the Ocean Routes to the Island; a Handbook for Travelers, with 2 Specially Drawn Maps and 7 Plans.* Houghton Mifflin, 1926.

Ukers, William Harrison: *All About Coffee.* Tea and Coffee Trade Journal Company, 1922, p. 8.

The Nordics

Albala, Ken: *Food Cultures of the World Encyclopedia.* Greenwood, 2011, p. 313.

Åreng, Emil: *Kaffekask—Från råtypisk Nationaldryck till Lyxdrink.* Kafferosteriet Koppar AB, 4 Mar. 2019, www.kafferosterietkoppar.se/info/proffsets-kaffekask-recept/> (accessed 6 June 2021)

Brones, A., and Kindvall, J.: *Fika: The Art of the Swedish Coffee Break, with Recipes for Pastries, Breads, and Other Treats.* Ten Speed Press, 2015, p. 3.

Cederström, B.M.: *Folkloristic koinés and the emergence of Swedish-American ethnicity.* Arv, Nordic Yearbook of Folklore, V. 68, 2012, pp. 121–150.

Charrier, André, and Berthaud, Julien: *Botanical Classification of Coffee.* In: *Coffee: Botany, Biochemistry and Production of Beans and Beverage,* ed. by M.N. Clifford and K.C. Willson, The AVI Publishing Company, Inc., 1985, pp. 13–47.

Dregni, Eric: *Vikings in the Attic: In Search of Nordic America*. University of Minnesota Press, 2013.

Fox, Killian: *The Gannet's Gastronomic Miscellany*. Octopus, 2017.

Harbutt, Juliet: *World Cheese Book*. DK Publishing, 2015, p. 251.

Hatt, Emilie Demant, and Sjoholm, Barbara: *With the Lapps in the High Mountains: a Woman among the Sami, 1907–1908*. The University of Wisconsin Press, 2013.

Hodacs, Hanna: *4 Coffee and Coffee Surrogates in Sweden: A Local, Global, and Material History*. In: *Locating the Global*, ed. by Holger Weiss, De Gruyter Oldenbourg, 2020, pp. 73–94, DOI: 10.1515/9783110670714-004 (accessed 13 May 2021).

Koerner, Lisbet: *Linnaeus: Nature and Nation*. Harvard University Press, 2009, p. 130.

Kolbu, Chris, and Wuolab, Anne: *Saami Coffee Culture*. In: *Indigenous Efflorescence: Beyond Revitalisation in Sapmi and Ainu Mosir*, ed. by Gerald Roche et al., ANU Press, 2018, pp. 205–208, JSTOR, www.jstor.org/stable/j.ctv9hj9pb.32 (accessed 19 May 2021).

Lagerholm, J.: *Hemmets läkarebok, populär medicinsk rådgifvare för friska och sjuka: med över 200 illustrationer en mångfald färgtrycksplanscher samt 5 isärtagbara modeller, receptbok till bruk för hemmet, ordlista över medicinska termer ock uttryck, förslag till husapotek, stort uppslagsregister*. Fröléen, 1924, p. 212.

Lintelman, Joy K.: *A Hot Heritage: Swedish Americans and Coffee*. Minnesota History, 63/5, Spring 2013, pp. 190–202.

Müller, Leos: *Kolonialprodukter i Sveriges handel och konsumtionskultur, 1700–1800*. Historisk tidskrift, 124, 2004, pp. 225–248.

Rolnick, Harry: *The Complete Book of Coffee*. Melitta, 1986, p. 76.

Ukers, William Harrison: *All About Coffee*. Tea and Coffee Trade Journal Company, 1922, p. 290.

Perry, Sara: *The New Complete Coffee Book: A Gourmet Guide to Buying, Brewing, and Cooking*. Chronicle Books, 2003.

Preedy, Victor: *Coffee in Health and Disease Prevention*. Elsevier Science, 2014, p. 266.

Reindeer Cheese. Ark of Taste. Slow Food Foundation for Biodiversity, www.fondazioneslowfood.com/en/ark-of-taste-slow-food/reindeer-cheese (accessed 21 May 2021).

Samisk mat. Exempel på mattraditioner som grund för det moderna samiska köket. The Sami Parliament, May 2010, www.samer.se/3539 (accessed 21 May 2021).

Sider, Gerald M.: *Skin for Skin: Death and Life for Inuit and Innu*. Duke University Press, 2014, p. 5.

Sønderjysk Kaffebord. Visit Sønderjylland, 2021, www.visitsonderjylland.dk/turist/oplevelser/en-bid-af-soenderjylland/soenderjysk-kaffebord (accessed 15 June 2021).

Wright, George Frederick, and Upham, Warren: *Greenland Icefields and Life in the North Atlantic: With a New Discussion of the Causes of the Ice Age*. K. Paul, Trench, Trübner & Company Limited, 1896, p. 130.

Turkey

Collaço, Gwendolyn: *The Ottoman Coffeehouse: All the Charms and Dangers of Commonality in the 16th-17th Centuries*. Lights: The MESSA Journal, A University of Chicago Graduate Publication 1, No. 1 (Fall 2011), pp. 61–71.

Gokce, Yesim: *Your Future in a Cup of Coffee*. Turkish Cultural Foundation www.turkishculture.org/lifestyles/turkish-culture-portal/coffee-fortune-telling-205.htm (accessed 12 May 2021).

Howard, Douglas A.: *A History of the Ottoman Empire*. Cambridge University Press, 2017.

Kafadar, C.: *How Dark is the History of the Night, How Black the Story of Coffee, How Bitter the Tale of Love: The Changing Measure of Leisure and Pleasure in Early Modern Istanbul*. In: *Medieval and Early Modern Performance in the Eastern Mediterranean*, ed. by A. Öztürkmen and E.B. Vitz, Turnhout: Brepols, 2014, pp. 243–269, DOI:10.1484/M.LMEMS-EB.6.09070802050003050406090109 (accessed 12 May 2021).

Karababa, Emİnegül, and Ger, Gülİz: *Early Modern Ottoman Coffeehouse Culture and the Formation of the Consumer Subject*. Journal of Consumer Research, vol. 37, no. 5, 2011, pp. 737–760, JSTOR, www.jstor.org/stable/10.1086/656422 (accessed 25 May 2021)

Kritzeck, James: *Anthology of Islamic Literature, From the Rise of Islam to Modern Times*. Holt, Rinehart, and Winston, 1964, pp. 326–334.

Lafferty, Samantha: *Istanbul & Surroundings Travel Adventures*. Hunter Publishing, Incorporated, 2011.

Malecka, A.: *How Turks and Persians Drank Coffee: A Little-known Document of Social History*. Turkish Historical Review, 6 (2), 2015, pp. 175–193, DOI: 10.1163/18775462-00602006 (accessed 12 May 2021).

Osmanoğlu, Ayşe, and Ünüvar, Safiye: *The Hazenidar Ustas and Hazenidar Kalfas*. In: *The Concubine, the Princess, and the Teacher: Voices from the Ottoman Harem*, by Douglas Scott Brookes, University of Texas Press, 2010, p. 236.

Peçevi, Ibrahim: *Tarih-I*. In: *Istanbul and the Civilization of the Ottoman Empire*, by Bernard Lewis,University of Oklahoma Press, 1963, 133.

Shaw, Ezel Kural, and Shaw, Stanford J.: *History of the Ottoman Empire and Modern Turkey: Volume 1, Empire of the Gazis: The Rise and Decline of the Ottoman Empire 1280–1808*. Cambridge University Press, 1976.

Yaccob, Abdol Rauh: *Yemeni Opposition to Ottoman Rule: an Overview*. Proceedings of the Seminar for Arabian Studies, vol. 42, 2012, pp. 411–419, JSTOR, www.jstor.org/stable/41623653 (accessed 11 May 2021).

Vietnam

Agergaard, Jytte, Fold, Niels, and Gough, Katherine: *Global-Local Interactions: Socioeconomic and Spatial Dynamics in Vietnam's Coffee Frontier*. The Geographical Journal, 175, 2009, pp. 133–145, DOI: 10.1111/j.1475-4959.2009.00320.x. (accessed 21 May 2021).

Bouillet, Marie Nicolas: *Cafetière*. In: *Dictionnaire universel des sciences, des lettres et des arts: avec l'explication et l'étymologie de tous les termes techn., l'histoire sommaire de chacune des principales branches des connaissances humaines, et l'indication des principaux ouvrages qui s'y rapportent*. Hachette, 1855, p. 234.

Coste, Jean-François: *Almanach des gourmands: servant de guide dans les moyens de faire excellente chere*. Vol. 2, Chez Maradan, 1805, p. 212.

D'haeze, Dave & Deckers, Jozef & Raes, Dirk & Phong, T.A. & Loi, H.: *Environmental and Socio-Economic Impacts of Institutional Reforms on the Agricultural Sector of Vietnam Land Suitability Assessment for Robusta Coffee in the Dak Gan Region*. Agriculture, Ecosystems & Environment, 105, 2005, pp. 59–76, DOI: 10.1016/j.agee.2004.05.009 (accessed 21 May 2021).

Doutriaux, S., Geisler, C. and Shively, G.: *Competing for Coffee Space: Development-Induced Displacement in the Central Highlands of Vietnam*. Rural Sociology, 73, 2008, pp. 528–554, DOI: 10.1526/003601108786471422 (accessed 30 April 2021).

Goscha, Christopher: *Vietnam: A New History*. Basic Books, 2016, p. 157.

Heard, Brent & Trinh, Thi Huong & Burra, et al.: *The Influence of Household Refrigerator Ownership on Diets in Vietnam*. Economics & Human Biology, 39, DOI: 10.1016/j.ehb.2020.100930. (accessed 21 May 2021).

Marsh, Anthony: *Diversification by Smallholder Farmers: Viet Nam Robusta Coffee*. Food and Agriculture Organization of the United Nations, 2007.

McLeod, M.W., Dieu, N.T., Nguyen, T. D: *Culture and Customs of Vietnam*. Greenwood Press, 2001, p. 128.

Meyfroidt, p. et al.: *Trajectories of Deforestation, Coffee Expansion and Displacement of Shifting Cultivation in the Central Highlands of Vietnam*. Global Environmental Change-human and Policy Dimensions 23, 2013, pp. 1187–1198.

Nguyen, Thuy Linh: *Childbirth, Maternity, and Medical Pluralism in French Colonial Vietnam, 1880–1945*. University of Rochester Press, 2016, p. 160.

Peters, E.J.: *Appetites and Aspirations in Vietnam: Food and Drink in the Long Nineteenth Century*. AltaMira Press, 2012, p. 201.

Luna, Fátima, and Wilson, Paul N.: *An Economic Exploration of Smallholder Value Chains: Coffee Transactions in Chiapas, Mexico*. International Food and Agribusiness Management Review, vol. 18, issue 3, 2015, p. 87.

Yemen

Ficquet, Éloi: *Many Worlds in a Cup: Identity Transactions in the Legend of Coffee Origins*. L'Africa Nel Mondo, Il Mondo in Africa/Africa in the World, the World in Africa. Ed. A. Gori and F. Viti. Milano: Accademia Ambrosiana, 2021.

Giovannucci, Daniele: *Moving Yemen Coffee Forward Assessment of the Coffee Industry in Yemen to Sustainably Improve Incomes and Expand Trade*. USAID, pdf.usaid.gov/pdf_docs/Pnadf516.pdf (accessed 24 April 2021).

Hattox, Ralph S.: *Coffee and Coffeehouses: The Origins of a Social Beverage in the Medieval Near East*. University of Washington Press, 1985.

Introduction to the Archaeology of RAK. Department of Heritage Antiquities & Museum, Ras Al Khaimah, www.rakheritage.rak.ae/en/pages/intro.aspx (accessed 23 April 2021).

Montagnon, C., Mahyoub, A., Solano, W., and Sheibani, F.: *Unveiling a Unique Genetic Diversity of Cultivated Coffea Arabica L. in its Main Domestication Center: Yemen*. Genetic Resources and Crop Evolution, 2021, link.springer.com/article/10.1007/s10722-021-01139-y (accessed 22 April 2021).

Robinette, G.W.: *The War on Coffee*. Graffiti Militante Press, 2018, p. 147.

Walker, Bethany J., Insoll, Timothy, and Fenwick, Corisande: *The Oxford Handbook of Islamic Archaeology*. Oxford University Press, 2020, p. 204.

Kafadarpp, Cemal: *How Dark is the History of the Night, How Black the Story of Coffee, How Bitter the Tale of Love: The Changing Measure of Leisure and Pleasure in Early Modern Istanbul*. In: *Medieval and Early Modern Performance in the Eastern Mediterranean*, Brepols Publishers, 2014, pp. 243–269.

Ukers, William Harrison: *All About Coffee*. Tea and Coffee Trade Journal Company, 1922, p. 26.

Wild, Antony: *Coffee: A Dark History*. W W Norton & Co Inc, 2005, p. 76.

Yaccob, Abdol Rauh: *Yemeni opposition to Ottoman rule: an overview*. Proceedings of the Seminar for Arabian Studies Vol. 42, Papers from the forty-fifth meeting of the Seminar for Arabian Studies held at the British Museum, London, 28 to 30 July 2011, 2012, pp. 411–419.

PICTURE CREDITS AND EXPERTS

Introduction

Our Food Stories, ourfoodstories.com
p. 5

Gunvor Eline Eng Jakobsen, gunvorejakobsen.no
p. 6

David Post, david-post.com
p. 9

Elena Shamis, elensham.com
p. 23

Italy

Elena Shamis, elensham.com
pp. 27–28, 31 (top), 33

Gentl & Hyers, gentlandhyers.com
pp. 31 (bottom), 32

Adam Smigielski, gettyimages
p. 35

REDA&CO, gettyimages
p. 37

Gunvor Eline Eng Jakobsen, gunvorejakobsen.no
pp. 39, 41

Ethiopia

David Post, david-post.com
pp. 43–44, 47 (top)

Eric Lafforgue, ericlafforgue.com
pp. 46, 47 (bottom), 51, 55

Ian Willms, ianwillms.com
pp. 49, 53

Tanzania

Gunvor Eline Eng Jakobsen gunvorejakobsen.no
pp. 57–58, 61, 63

Jake Lyell, Alamy Stock Photo
p. 60

Yemen

Sabcomeed, sabcomeed.com
p. 65

Mohammed Hamoud, gettyimages
p. 66

Narinnate Mekkajorn, Alamy Stock Photo
p. 69

Arabian Peninsula

Eric Lafforgue, ericlafforgue.com
pp. 71, 72 (top)

StockphotoVideo, Alamy Stock Photo
p. 72 (bottom)

Caroline Ericson, Alamy Stock Photo
p. 74

by Marc Guitard, gettyimages
p. 75

FabrikaCr, gettyimages
p. 77

christophe cappelli, Alamy Stock Photo
p. 79

Turkey

Luis Dafos, Alamy Stock Photo
p. 81

David Towers, Alamy Stock Photo
p. 82 (top)

Katrina Frederick, katrinafrederick.com
pp. 82 (bottom), 87

Inna Finkova, Alamy Stock Photo
p. 84

Dermot Blackburn, Alamy Stock Photo
p. 85

India

travelib kerala, Alamy Stock Photo
p. 89

Chris Schalkx, ricepotato.co
pp. 90, 95

imageBROKER, Alamy Stock Photo
p. 92

Sugato Mukherjee, Alamy Stock Photo
p. 93 (top)

Photo by Jogesh S, gettyimages
p. 93 (bottom)

Reza, gettyimages
p. 94

Beatrix Basu, beatrixbasu.com
pp. 97, 99, 101

Indonesia

Elena Shamis, elensham.com
pp. 103 (top), 104, 107, 109

Alana Dimou, alanadimou.com
pp. 103 (bottom), 108

David Hagerman, davidhagermanphoto.com
p. 106

Beatrix Basu, beatrixbasu.com
pp. 111, 115

Gunvor Eline Eng Jakobsen, gunvorejakobsen.no
pp. 113, 117

Spain

Alana Dimou, alanadimou.com
pp. 119, 120 (top), 122–123, 125

Jerónimo Alba, Alamy Stock Photo
p. 120 (bottom)

Petr Svarc, Alamy Stock Photo
p. 124 (top)

Michael Brooks, Alamy Stock Photo
p. 124 (bottom)

Gunvor Eline Eng Jakobsen, gunvorejakobsen.no
p. 127

ImagesbyK, gettyimages
p. 129

Beatrix Basu, beatrixbasu.com
p. 131

Caribbean

agefotostock, Alamy Stock Photo
p. 133 (top)

All Canada Photos, Alamy Stock Photo
p. 133 (bottom)

Jon Arnold Images Ltd, Alamy Stock Photo
pp. 134, 136, 138 (top)

Elijah-Lovkoff, gettyimages
p. 137

Carlos Sala Fotografia, Shutterstock
p. 138 (bottom)

Terry Donnelly, Alamy Stock Photo
p. 139

Gunvor Eline Eng Jakobsen, gunvorejakobsen.no
p. 141, 143

Brazil

Ian Trower, Alamy Stock Photo
p. 145

Jair Ferreira Belafacce, Shutterstock
p. 146 (top)

Deni Williams, Alamy Stock Photo
p. 146 (bottom)

Cavan Images, Alamy Stock Photo
p. 148

Graham Mulrooney, Alamy Stock Photo
p. 149 (top)

Zoonar GmbH, Alamy Stock Photo
p. 149 (bottom)

T photography, Shutterstock
p. 151

Mexico

Kamira, Alamy Stock Photo
p. 153 (top)

Marcos Castillo, Alamy Stock Photo
p. 153 (bottom)

Bjanka Kadic, Alamy Stock Photo
p. 154

Ingrid Hofstra, ingridhofstra.com
p. 156

Ed Rooney, Alamy Stock Photo
p. 157 (top)

Jesse Kraft, Alamy Stock Photo
p. 157 (bottom)

Gunvor Eline Eng Jakobsen, gunvorejakobsen.no
p. 159

©fitopardo, gettyimages
p. 161

Polynesia

Kritsada Petchuay, gettyimages
p. 163 (top)

Andre Jenny, Alamy Stock Photo
p. 163 (bottom)

Russ Bishop, Alamy Stock Photo
p. 164

Adam Hester, gettyimages
p. 166

Derek Brown, Alamy Stock Photo
p. 167 (top)

Dave G. Houser, Alamy Stock Photo
p. 167 (bottom)

Gunvor Eline Eng Jakobsen, gunvorejakobsen.no
p. 169

Japan

Ingrid Hofstra, ingridhofstra.com
p. 171

Alana Dimou, alanadimou.com
pp. 172–179, 189

MAKI STUDIO, Alamy Stock Photo
p. 181

Abdulrahman, EyeEm, g ettyimages
p. 183

horst friedrichs, Alamy Stock Photo
p. 185

Gunvor Eline Eng Jakobsen, gunvorejakobsen.no
p. 187

Vietnam

Samuel Dowal-Asselin, mappingalong.com
pp. 191, 195 (top)

David Hagerman, davidhagermanphoto.com
pp. 192–194, 195 (bottom)

NhatTienLe, gettyimages
p. 197

Gunvor Eline Eng Jakobsen, gunvorejakobsen.no
p. 199

Linh Moran Photography, gettyimages
p. 201

Beatrix Basu, beatrixbasu.com
p. 203

Singapore

Gunvor Eline Eng Jakobsen, gunvorejakobsen.no
pp. 205–206

Photographed by PhotostOry, gettyimages
p. 209

Beatrix Basu, beatrixbasu.com
p. 211

Korea

Jen Kim, aretherelilactrees.com
pp. 213–216, 217 (top), 218–221

Inhee Jjang/EyeEm, Alamy Stock Photo
p. 217 (bottom)

Gunvor Eline Eng Jakobsen, gunvorejakobsen.no
p. 223

Andria Lo, andrialo.com
p. 225

Austria, Germany, Switzerland

Gianluca Fazio, gettyimages
p. 227

Patricia Weisskirchner, patriciaweisskirchner.com
pp. 228 (oben), 235, 239, 243

Giannis Papanikos, Shutterstock
p. 228 (unten)

Pavel Dudek, Alamy Stock Foto
p. 231 (oben)

Maridav, Shutterstock
p. 231 (unten)

Stefano Politi Markovina, Alamy Stock Foto
p. 232

Kirill Livshitskiy, Shutterstock
p. 233 (oben)

marcobrivio.photo, Shutterstock
p. 233 (unten))

Tohuwabohu1976, Shutterstock
p. 237

jejejune, Shutterstock
p. 241

The Nordics

Gunvor Eline Eng Jakobsen, gunvorejakobsen.no
pp. 245, 251, 254 (top), 255–259

Elena Shamis, elensham.com
p. 246

David Post, david-post.com
pp. 249–250, 252–253

Pawel Garski, Alamy Stock Photo
p. 254 (bottom)

Charlie Bennet, charliebennet.com
p. 261

Glossary

Gunvor Eline Eng Jakobsen, gunvorejakobsen.no
pp. 255

David Post, david-post.com
pp. 256

EXPERTS

This book would not have been possible without the advice of the following experts who reviewed, translated, edited, and provided insights about the coffee culture and traditions in their countries of expertise

Arabian Peninsula

Anda Greeney
Master's Candidate, Harvard University, Yemen's contemporary and historical coffee sector; owner of Al Mokha online coffee shop

Abdullah Bin Nasser Bin Kulayb
Qahwa championships judge; Co-Founder of Knoll Coffee Roasters and Kooz Al Qahwa Coffee Roasters in Saudi Arabia

Youness Marour and Olivia Curl
Arabic Translation

Brazil

Dr. Seth W. Garfield
Professor, Brazilian history and environmental history, The University of Texas at Austin

Ethiopia

Dr. Éloi Ficquet
Anthropologist and historian; Professor at the EHESS School for Advanced Studies in the Social Sciences in Paris; Director of the French Center for Ethiopian Studies in Addis Ababa; author of A French-Amharic Dictionary

Japan

Dr. Merry White
Professor of Anthropology at Boston University, with specialties in Japanese studies, food, and travel; Author of Coffee Life in Japan

India

Dr. Bhaswhati Bhattacharya
Author of Much Ado About Coffee and former Research Fellow in Indian Social History Department at University of Göttingen

Indonesia

Adi Taroepratjeka
Host of Coffee Story Show, Indonesia's first Q Grader, Coffee Educator

Korea

Dr. Jia Choi
Food culture researcher, historian, and consultant, PhD in Food & Nutrition, Ewha University, Seoul

Jung Gee
Editor of Coffee Monthly, Korea

Mexico

Dr Steffan Igor Ayora Diaz
Professor of Anthropology, Universidad Autónoma de Yucatán

Dr. Casey Lurtz
Assistant Professor in History, Johns Hopkins University; author of From the Grounds Up: Building an Export Economy in Southern Mexico

The Nordics

Linda Sandvik
Former employee of Nordic Approach

Polynesia

Shawn Steiman
Coffee consultant, Hawai'i

Singapore

Dr. Khairudin Aljunied
Associate Professor of Intellectual and Social History of the Malay World, National University of Singapore

Robert Chohan
Owner of Kopi House, UK

Spain

Kim Ossenblok
Coffee consultant and writer, author of ¡AL GRANO!

Tanzania

Dr. Ned Bertz
Associate Professor of South Asia, Africa, Indian Ocean, World History, University of Hawai'i

Noreen Chichon and Thomas Plattner
Coffee professionals at Zanzibar Coffee Company/Utengule Estates

Turkey

Dr. Hakan Karateke
Professor of Ottoman and Turkish Culture, Language and Literature, The University of Chicago

Vietnam

Erica J. Peters
Culinary historian; author of Appetites and Aspirations in Vietnam: Food and Drink in the Long Nineteenth Century; co-founder and director of the Culinary Historians of Northern California

Tr'ần Hân
Vietnam's National Barista Champion

Yemen

Faris Sheibani
Yemen-focused green coffee trader and founder of Qima Coffee

Anda Greeney
Master's Candidate, Harvard University, Yemen's contemporary and historical coffee sector; owner of Al Mokha online coffee shop

Spill the Beans

GLOBAL COFFEE CULTURE AND RECIPES

Lani Kingston

This book was edited and designed by gestalten.

Contributing editor: Lani Kingston

Concept, text, and recipes by Lani Kingston
Recipe testing and editing by Rachel V Kingston
Captions by Anna Southgate

Edited by Robert Klanten and Andrea Servert

Editorial Management by Lars Pietzschmann

Head of Design: Niklas Juli
Cover, design and layout by Stefan Morgner

Photo Editor: Madeline Dudley-Yates
Cover photography by Our Food Stories
(Laura Muthesius & Nora Eisermann)
Back cover image by Elena Shamis

Illustrations by David Sparshott (pp. 10–21, 24–25)

Typefaces: Mencken by Jean François Porchez,
Kaftan by Victor Bartis

Printed by Print Best, Viljandi
Made in Europe

Published by gestalten, Berlin 2025
Updated Edition
1st printing, 2025
ISBN 978-3-96704-203-0

Die Gestalten Verlag GmbH & Co. KG
Mariannenstrasse 9–10
10999 Berlin, Germany
hello@gestalten.com

For more information, and to order books, please visit www.gestalten.com

Bibliographic information published by the Deutsche Nationalbibliothek. The Deutsche Nationalbibliothek lists this publication in the Deutsche Nationalbibliografie; detailed bibliographic data is available online at www.dnb.de

None of the content in this book was published in exchange for payment by commercial parties or designers; gestalten selected all included work based solely on its artistic merit.

This book was printed on paper certified according to the standards of the FSC®.